D0915661

Liliana's
Journal

LILIANA ZUKER-BUJANOWSKA

Liliana's Journal:

Warsaw 1939-1945

THE DIAL PRESS   NEW YORK

Published by
The Dial Press
1 Dag Hammarskjold Plaza
New York, New York 10017

Manufactured in the United States of America

First printing

Design by Oksana Kushnir

Library of Congress Cataloging in Publication Data

Zuker-Bujanowska, Liliana, 1928–
Liliana's journal.

Translated from Polish.
1. Holocaust, Jewish (1939–1945)—Poland—Warsaw—
Personal narratives.   2.   Zuker-Bujanowska, Liliana,
1928–   3.   Jews in Warsaw—Biography.   4.   Warsaw—
Biography.   I.   Title.
D810.J4Z8413   943.8′053′0924 [B]   80–139
ISBN 0-8037-4997-X

I want to dedicate this book to the memory of my parents, Emilia Anna and Stefan.

I want to thank my sister-in-law Nell. Without her faith in my ability to translate this book and a little push from time to time, I could not have done it.

AUTHOR'S NOTE

Dear Readers, this book is a picture of seven years of my life. My hope was to give you the most truthful and objective story possible of this part of my existence. I skipped only the facts that could endanger the lives of my friends who are still living in the world behind the wall. I changed the names of some people and some places.

I hope you will forgive me for the errors I made translating this book from Polish to English. I have lived in this country for over twenty years. I still speak with an accent that my friends call cute, and my grammar is not the best. War was my place of learning and German soldiers were my teachers.

My eternal thanks go to my uncle and aunt, Mr. and Mrs. Ladislao Cukier. They live in San Salvador in the Republic of El Salvador in Central America. When I arrived in New York, all the papers for my final destination, El Salvador, were waiting for me. The Cukiers were the only family I had left and they wanted me to live with them. They received me in their home like one of their children. I had a peaceful and happy life there.

For the first few months, because I did not speak Spanish, I was a little bored. I took lessons for an hour every day, but could only communicate in Polish with my uncle and aunt. Their children, Sofie, age eight, and Mike, age four, and the house help spoke only Spanish. I therefore decided to spend all my free time writing down everything I could remember about the preceding seven years of my life.

I finished writing in about six months, and by then I could communicate in Spanish pretty well, met a lot of people my age, and put these pages away, stacked in a nice, clean box tied with a ribbon in the bottom drawer.

Liliana's Journal

chapter **1**

*I*t was a beautiful August day and the sun had started its journey to the west. I could see its reddish-yellow face peeking through the tall trees and slowly disappearing behind the horizon. Dusk in the small Polish village was enchanting. I loved this time of day, and I loved this time of year—it was vacation time, away from the city, away from school.

Civilization had not affected the life of the Polish farmer. The little houses were as primitive as they must have been years and years ago, with no running water, with outside toilets—far away from the house—and thatched roofs. The homes of the more prosperous farmers stood out—their roofs were covered with tiles. But all of them were clean, painted white, with flower gardens and white picket fences. Passing by them you could smell the aroma of fresh-baked bread. They were good people, happy to make some extra money during the summer months when townspeople like ourselves came to the nearby resorts. The townspeople went to the village often to buy fresh vegetables, butter, thick and creamy buttermilk (the most popular beverage), and the best fresh cheese.

While the older folks were buying, we children tasted. The farmer's wife was always ready to give the children big slices of fresh wheat bread spread with the best-smelling butter and a little salt on the top. If this was not enough to satisfy our enormous appetites, there were apples and pears on the trees nearby. "Pick as many as you can eat," said the lady farmer. "The ones with the red cheeks are the ripe ones."

I had just come home from that kind of feast, and I think I had eaten too many apples. I felt like I was going to explode. I was tired and all I could think about was to lie under my favorite oak tree and dream. I could feel the gentle breeze caressing my face, blowing through my hair, and in my imagination, whispering in my ear, "Don't worry, little girl, you ate too much, but tomorrow you will feel fine . . . you are young, life is wonderful . . . and use every minute of it to beautify it even more . . . even if it means eating too much."

I don't know how long I had been lying there, so completely immobile, when suddenly I heard my friend calling. " 'Turkey' is coming! Can't you hear 'turkey' is coming!"

I heard it too as it stopped in front of our house. My father had arrived in his red car. We all called it turkey, though I am not quite sure why. Maybe because it was bright red, maybe because it made a funny noise, or maybe because it was rather ugly.

I got up as fast as I could and ran to greet my father. I did not think for a moment how strange it was for him to come during the week. He always came on Friday night and stayed until Monday morning. Papa kissed me gently on the cheek and entered the house, and I ran to join my friends.

It was almost an hour before dinner, a whole hour to play. Only two weeks were left before we had to be back in the city and school. I had a lot of friends in this summer place. We had been coming here for the past five years, and we always rented an apartment in this house. It was a villa with two apartments on the first floor and two on the second floor. The year before we had rented the whole first floor, and the whole family spent the summer there, including both my grandmothers, my uncle Josef (on mother's side), and his wife Lula. She was the most beautiful one in the whole family. She had long black hair and the bluest eyes I had ever seen. Those who worked came on weekends, and with people coming and going all the time, it really was fun.

This year we had an apartment on the second floor. Just below us lived a family with two grown-up sons, Steve and Anek. They were college-age boys, and I had a crush on Steve from the moment I laid eyes on him. He was tall and handsome, but all he did was pat me on my head when we met in the hall. I did not worry too much about it; I had a perfect play companion, Alik Kutnowski. He always played the games I wanted to play, and we both organized all kinds of activities for our little group. Bicycle riding—rest—a game of croquet—rest—and we walked miles in the fields picking wild flowers. And then it was lunch or dinner time and nobody suffered from a lack of appetite. Autumn was almost here, we could smell the hay drying in the field. The best way to pick the wild flowers was to walk not too far behind the farmer when he was cutting the wheat. The flowers that survived his sharp machete we gathered and took home to our mothers. There were bluebells, bachelor's buttons, and poppies—my favorite.

In the afternoons, the whole family went to the woods to gather mushrooms. We all picked only *prawdziwki*—they are the best to dry. We took them home, cleaned and cut them, then put them on the strings to dry, and we had enough for the whole winter.

After Papa came, Alik asked me what kind of news Father had brought from the city. I did not know what kind of news the adults were talking about and was not especially interested. I was only eleven years old. But I decided to go home and find out.

I found everybody on the terrace talking very fast, and their faces looked somber. They were so deeply engrossed in the conversation that they did not notice my presence. The word I heard over and over again was "war"! I was aware enough to know that it was serious and I thought I knew what the word "war" meant. They said that Hitler had signed the pact with Russia, that after taking Austria and Czechoslovakia, he wanted the Polish "corridor"—a strip of land on the north and the only access to the Baltic Sea.

During dinner the conversation was very serious, with none of the usual jokes. Mother and Father looked at each other, and Grandmother Helena looked at me somewhat strangely, as though it were my fault that the war was hanging over our heads.

I had learned a lot about wars in Polish history. Poland had lived through many wars in her ancient history, but now——

Papa, as usual, was very optimistic. He did not believe that war would actually break out. But for the safety of the family it was decided to leave for the city, where we would pack what we could and go east. Our city, Kalisz, was in the western half of the country, and they decided that somewhere to the east would be safer.

The next day we left the beautiful vacation land for the hot city of Kalisz.

chapter 2

*O*nce we returned to Kalisz, everyone started immediately to pack everything. All the china and crystal was packed in crates and put in the basement. Some clothes, blankets, linens, and pillows were sent to friends in Warsaw.

People on the streets walked around in a daze. Nobody knew what to do, what was the right thing to do, where to go and what to take along.

The day before we were to leave Kalisz, my parents took me to a place where they buried a glass jar full of jewelry. They wanted everybody in the family to know exactly where it was. I felt so grown up! The "big" folks had shared their secret with me. At the same time I felt that my wonderful, trouble-free past was being buried in this little glass jar.

That was August 24, 1939. A day later Grandmother Helena and Grandfather Max and I left for Naleczow.

Naleczow was a well-known summer resort, beautifully situated on small hills covered with green forest, and supposedly safe, because it lay in what was at that time the heart of Poland. My parents and Grandmother Maria (on Father's side) stayed behind. Father was waiting to be called to the army. He was an officer in the reserve, and they were supposed to be called first. Mother did not want to leave him, and *Babcia* Maria had plans to go to Warsaw.

The trip to Naleczow was like a bad dream. The train was full of men trying to report to their army units. It was very hard to get inside the train and impossible to get a seat. All the young men were singing patriotic songs, including our national anthem, *Jeszcze Polska nie zginela*. Here and there somebody shouted, "Kill Hitler—hang him by his——!" Why that way, I did not understand. All this gave us a little taste of the prewar activities. We had to change trains in Warsaw, and waited for hours, sitting on our suitcases, for the right connection. I don't know how long we had been sitting there, when Grandma met a young man from Kalisz. He was going to join his regiment in Lublin and he helped us to get on the train and load our luggage. Lublin was a bit east of Naleczow.

Finally, Naleczow. I imagined it to be a wonderful town, the place where we were to stay safely and quietly while the war raged all around us (if the war did break out). Naleczow was supposedly the safest place possible. It was situated far from train lines, had no military installations, and was in the center of the country.

Well, it did not turn out to be so. The dreamland turned out to be hell. We found a small room in a small inn. The food was terrible, but the worst were the nights. The beds were full of bedbugs. We stayed up all night with flashlights, trying to kill as many as we could. By day Naleczow was a charming little town whose center was a big park with beautiful fountains and colorful flower beds. The water had some kind of medicinal value, and everybody sat around the fountains drinking it from little glasses with straws. We took long walks in the park, drank the water, and tried not to think about the nights, with those ugly little creatures await-ing us in the darkness.

Four days passed. I was waiting for Mother. My grand-parents were very good to me, but nobody could replace my mother. They took good care of me, but were so busy reading newspapers and listening to the radio that I was left alone with my own thoughts.

Then came September 1, 1939, the date Poland and the world will never forget. From that day on the blood of Polish soldiers, women, and children flowed. Modern cities, full of life, built during the twenty-year period of Polish indepen-dence, were crushed and all that remained was rubble.

I awakened that day thinking that school would start soon and that my birthday, September 20, the day we always celebrated so lavishly, was close. With my eyes still shut I thought about what I would like to have for my birthday. Then the door burst open and my grandfather ran in waving a small newspaper. "Special edition—extra—war with Germany!" That was September 1, only hours before German tanks crossed the border.

For a moment I felt like my head was suddenly empty; all the blood had stopped somewhere before it reached the brain. I was too frightened to open my mouth and ask about Mother. Where is she? Why isn't she here with me? What will happen to me? I closed my eyes and started to pray. All kinds of thoughts crossed my mind. "Maybe my mother was killed? Oh, God. Then take me too. I do not want to live without her a day, an hour, not even a minute." I prayed so hard that I was sure whatever I asked for, God would grant me, and I felt better.

The hall downstairs was like a beehive, with people running back and forth. Men did not know what to do—should they stay or run? The radio was blasting coded messages and instructions to the citizens on how to behave in case of air attack. All this "news" only terrified people more. Homeowners wanted to build air-raid shelters, but it was too late for that.

The same afternoon my mother arrived, tired and dirty,

but happy. My mother had come to me—my prayers were answered. She had left Kalisz two days before. Father had stayed behind, still waiting for his papers. Mother was able to go by train to Warsaw, but from there all the trains had been requisitioned by the army, and she had taken a taxi all the way to Naleczow. That in itself was a miracle, because the army was commandeering any car they could get. The trip took five hours. I was so happy—my mother had done all that to be with us—with me! Now I did not care if the world crumbled, I did not care if the bedbugs were still biting at night—I had my mother with me.

After five days the Polish government, military and civilian, left Warsaw for a safer place: Naleczow. All the civilians were ordered to leave town in twelve hours. Everyone tried to find a place to sleep in the surrounding villages. We ran from farmer to farmer pleading for a space on the floor, but at every house we were just a little too late. The day was almost over when we found a place. It was about two kilometers from Naleczow, a small empty cabin without doors or windows but with one luxury: a roof. It had one bed and we let Grandma sleep in it. We slept on our luggage. The place was full of bugs, but I slept deeply after running all day.

A few days later the government moved farther east. Hour after hour the news grew worse, until finally the radio went silent and newspapers were no longer printed. People got news from other people. Nobody knew how accurate it was. Whatever the news, it was worse than we could have imagined. The Germans had taken all the little towns around Warsaw and were closing in on the city. Some divisions were moving east of the river Wisla. Everyone gathered a few belongings and fled farther east.

After long discussions we decided to go to Lublin, which was almost straight east from Naleczow. Mama rented a horse and wagon from a farmer, and with another family (who had relatives in Lublin) we moved east. We could only travel by night. During the day German planes machine-gunned everything that moved on the highways. It was a beautiful, bright, and warm early fall night.

The traffic on the road was chaotic. There were endless rows of horses and wagons on both sides with groups of soldiers on foot or horseback in the middle, all fleeing east. It was panic, with screams, families separated, mothers running around looking for their children. People wanted to move faster but couldn't. Some were angry and just pushed others around.

Far off we could see smoke rising from burning villages and we could hear explosions. That was the place we were running to? I was very frightened and thought we must be going in the wrong direction. We rode all night and stayed under clumps of trees during the day. As we neared Lublin it became worse, with more burning villages, more retreating soldiers, and more German planes trying to kill them. Every so often the traffic backed up and we just had to stop, sometimes between the walls of burning houses. The heat was terrible. The tongues of flame, pushed by the breeze, almost touched our wagon. One spark and all this hay we were sitting on could burn in a minute.

We sat in our wagon hugging each other for what I thought were hours. Soldiers on horseback tried to move faster, weaving in and out of the line of wagons, but they were stopped again and again by children running, looking for their parents, and people on foot carrying their belongings on their backs, moving very slowly.

We finally arrived in Lublin early in the morning. The streets were empty, and unusually quiet. We drove around for about an hour before we found the street where our friends' family lived. The building was large and untouched by bombs. Mother got off the wagon and knocked at the big wooden gate, once, twice, three times. Finally the door opened a crack and a man's face peered out. He was in charge of the security of this building and had orders not to let anybody in. "A lot of German spies around," he said.

Mother explained to him who we were, where we had

come from, that there were some old people and children in the wagon, and that "our cousins" lived here. Meanwhile we all got down from the wagon to stretch our legs. We were stiff from sitting so long. I sat down in the corner next to the gate and fell asleep immediately. Finally the man went inside looking for "our cousin Marta."

Marta received us all very warmly. Her apartment was full of people, family and strangers, like us. Mother asked her if she knew of a room we could rent for a few days. Marta stretched out her arms in desperation.

"Oh, my God, you want to stay in this hell. From morning to night German planes fly over the city and bomb it. The whole of Lublin is in rubble. Go, run farther east!"

We looked at her as though she was mad. It was so quiet. At any rate, we could not move any farther east because, my mother said, "Lilly and my parents just have to rest a day or two."

Marta gave us a space in the corner of her dining room to spread our blankets and sleep. One next to the other we put our heads down and I immediately fell asleep. I slept for about three hours, and then we all jumped up, awakened by several tremendous explosions. After the third one, plaster started to fall on our heads. Somewhere, somebody screamed, "To the shelter!" and we all ran. The apartment was on the third floor, and it was dangerous to stay. All the tenants had specific orders to get everybody to the shelter. Once we got downstairs it was impossible to enter the shelter. It was not big enough to hold the tenants as well as all the extra people in each apartment, and there were people who had lived in this basement for days now. They slept there, ate there, and little children used the corners as a toilet. It was a terrible place, full of dirt, stink, and screams.

With every explosion, and they sounded closer and closer, the people screamed louder. They were mostly women and children, hungry, dirty, nerves on edge, worrying about their husbands, fathers, and sons. Two women were nursing their babies, but they were so tired their arms could not hold the infants. When they rolled off their laps and started to cry, the mothers jumped and grabbed them back.

Suddenly a terrible explosion shook the air. The house swayed, glass shattered, and lumps of plaster started falling. Everyone just froze. I clung to Mother and started to cry.

After a few still minutes, the street filled with people. We heard banging at the front gate. The bomb had exploded across the street. Everybody ran, wanting to help, to save whatever they could from the burning house. They did not know what to save first. Some ran with pillows under their arms, one woman saved some towels and left behind a fur coat. Others left purses with money and saved old pots. They stared around without really seeing. After a while a few wounded came in. Somebody had a first aid kit and helped as much as he could. One young woman was holding a little boy in her arms; his face was scratched and bleeding a little. She held him very close and repeated over and over how happy she was that he did not have to go to the hospital. The Germans did not recognize any conventions. A red cross on a roof meant nothing. They were killing women and children working in the fields. Somebody told us a story about a little boy digging potatoes in the field who, when he saw the planes approaching, started to run to hide in the nearby forest, but the plane chased him across the fields until he dropped dead.

After that one day in Lublin we moved farther east to Chelm. It took us all night to get there. The only means of transportation was a horse and a very uncomfortable wooden wagon. The wagons were more and more difficult to find. Farmers were afraid to leave home and most of the horses had been taken by the army. The wagon we were able to rent was very narrow, with no hay, and the horse was very old and very slow. From far away we could hear the planes and heavy artillery.

Sometime during the night we heard that the Russian army had crossed the Polish border and was moving westward. This news disoriented the Polish army completely. Some said the Russians were coming to help us, others heard of skirmishes on the border. The officers did not know where to lead their detachments. Nobody knew where the general staff was. There were rumors that they had run toward Russia. Each officer did what he thought best. Some moved toward Rumania, others just dumped their uniforms and ran. Some wanted to go back to save Warsaw, but it was too late for that.

We knew Warsaw was completely surrounded, but we also knew that the city was still fighting. We all talked about Father. He was going to join us in Naleczow (oh, how far away it was), but to get there he would have to pass Warsaw. People who had been able to pass through reported that all the roads were covered with dead and wounded and there was nobody to bury the dead or help the wounded. All we could think about was, "When did he leave Kalisz? Did he have time enough to get to Warsaw before it was surrounded? Can he get out? Or is he somewhere on the road?"

The wagon moved slowly and its creaking put me to sleep.

We arrived in Chelm about 8 A.M. Mother went to look for a place for us to stay and we waited, walking around the wagon to stretch our weary bones. After almost an hour Mother came back smiling. She had found a nice, clean room. The most important details: it had two beds with clean linen.

For the first time in a week we washed and changed clothes, and our landlady brought us some fresh coffee. She was so nice and helpful, and very curious about the news from the west.

We slept the rest of that day and the whole night. The next morning Mother and I went to shop for some food, but every store in this town was closed. It was impossible even to buy a loaf of bread. People did not want Polish money; they would rather keep the merchandise. Our landlady shared with us whatever she had, mostly flour, so we lived on pancakes. We did not hear German planes or artillery; it was very quiet. We were sitting between two big powers moving toward each other, and we did not know what would happen when they met. After we had been waiting six days without any news from either side, Russian tanks entered the town of Chelm.

They came without firing a shot. The streets were empty for a short while, then some came out to welcome the soldiers, some even had flowers for them, others sat quietly behind closed doors and waited.

Soon thieves started to rob stores and empty houses. All of us helped to secure the front door with whatever wooden planks we could find. Within a few hours a whole Russian division with tanks and soldiers on foot poured into town. The soldiers looked tired, their coats were torn. The machine guns hung from their shoulders on their straps. Their faces were dirty and harsh-looking. The noise was unbelievable. The buildings shook. Curiosity overcame fear, and children began to run into the streets to look at these enormous machines. A few soldiers stopped and talked to the children, explaining how the machinery worked and asking where they could buy watches. They wanted to buy any kind of watch as long as it ticked.

The next day what we thought was a victory parade turned out to be a funeral for two soldiers killed near Chelm. The Russians dug a grave in the middle of town, covered it with red flowers, and put a red fence around it with a big red star in the middle.

A few days passed quietly and then people started to talk about a pact between the Germans and the Russians and how they had divided Poland between them. It was said that the Russians would pull back behind the Bug River. The Bug is a few kilometers to the east of Chelm. At first people did not pay too much attention to the rumors, but as the days passed they started to worry. Everyone seemed to want to stay with the Russians, especially those of us who were Jews. We knew, or thought we knew, what they had done with the German Jews. Later we learned that when they took Austria and Czechoslovakia, one of their first acts was to send all the Jews to the concentration camps.

Mother wanted to go with the Russians. But Grandfather Max wanted to go home to Kalisz. He did not care, he said, what they did to him. He wanted to die in his own bed. I did not realize it then, but he was becoming deranged. He walked around the room like a caged animal and from time to time screamed that he wanted to go home. Mother tried to persuade him and explain to him that he would never have the position that he had had before the war.

Grandfather had been a director of a paper manufacturing company. I loved to go to his factory and watch the machines make doilies in all kinds of patterns and sizes. It was fascinating the way the machine cut and rolled all colors of toilet paper. I liked the crêpe paper the best; I could take home scraps of different colors and make all kinds of things. Mother liked it too, because it occupied me for hours.

Nobody could change Grandfather's mind; he did not want to listen to reason. So the grown-ups decided that when we could, we would go back. Mother hoped to find Father somewhere around Warsaw or back home.

Several more days passed in nervous waiting.

"Will they stay?" "Will they leave?"

To all those preoccupations we had to add one more: food. The only thing we could buy was herring. Mother met and became friendly with a girl who worked in a military bakery, and every two or three days she would give us a few loaves of bread. So our everyday meals were bread and herring—Mother fixed them with onions and olive oil, and they were very good.

The Russians started to withdraw after ten days in Chelm. Big trucks rolled east day and night, full of furniture, machinery, food. They cleaned out all the government buildings and finally dug up the grave on the square and took their dead comrades with them. Then we knew for sure that the Germans were taking over this part of Poland. We could see numbers of young men and women with just a canvas bag on their shoulders, leaving the town. Very often the Russian trucks would stop and pick up a whole group of them. The last thing they moved out was the army hospital, the wounded and the personnel. They gave them a choice: stay with the Germans or go east to Russia. They provided all the help possible—ambulances for the sick and trucks for the rest.

We all stood there on the street and watched. Mother was very upset. She wanted to join the smart ones and run as far as she could from the ever-extending Germans' claws. If she had known then what the future had in store for us, she would not have listened to Grandfather.

The Russians left and with them most of the people. The town was quiet. We walked the streets trying to find some way to go west, toward home. One day we met a man Mother knew from Kalisz. Mr. Fajfer was the owner of a bus line in Kalisz that ran between the town and the railroad station. The whole family had run away in one of their buses and now were returning home. Mr. Fajfer said the bus was full, they had a lot of luggage, but he would take us. "Be ready in one hour," he said.

The bus was enormous—to me. It could seat thirty, but was so full of luggage that the nineteen people inside were very crowded. We drove for two hours and did not meet a soul, neither a German nor a Russian. The land was deserted.

About fifteen kilometers from Lublin we were stopped by a German border patrol.

"Who are you and where are you going?" asked the officer in charge.

The officer was not a young man. He had a pale, mean face. He asked for our papers. Everyone had to get off the bus and stand side by side in a long line. He did not like some of the documents and suddenly we heard the word "Jews." All the other soldiers turned to stare at us with curiosity mixed with hate. We had to take every piece of luggage off the bus for inspection. They supposedly were looking for ammunition, but took whatever they wanted. They told the men to line up on one side of the road, and women and children on the other. Screaming all the time, they pushed and kicked. It started to rain, an early morning drizzle, and wind blew through our wet clothes. It was cold and I was frightened. They continued for about an hour, kicking every open suitcase after they finished checking it, scattering clothes all over the road. That was the superior German race, the men that were going to rule Poland.

Suddenly one of the soldiers picked up Mrs. Fajfer's fur coat. He looked it over for a long while, as though he was trying to decide whether it was worth taking. Suddenly Mr. Fajfer took it out of his hand and pushed another suitcase forward to be checked. The German became furious. He screamed something in German and started to hit Mr. Fajfer in the face, again and again. Mr. Fajfer fell down. The German started to kick him with his heavy boots and then pulled his gun and pointed it at Mr. Fajfer's head. We all stopped breathing. One, two, three seconds passed. Suddenly the German started to laugh, like Satan's laugh. We expected the gun to fire, but we did not expect the laugh. It was a terrible sound, a sound that could kill, the sound of power without limits. They were our "masters."

After that incident another officer told us to have the bus loaded in three minutes, or he would shoot everybody. We all started to throw our belongings inside, and when the bus was full and started to move away, we followed it as briskly as we could without running or looking behind. After we lost sight of the Germans, we rearranged the luggage and climbed in. We arrived in Lublin that afternoon.

Mr. Fajfer wanted to buy gasoline and leave right away. But when we stopped at the gas station, people started to gather around us, asking all kinds of questions. On both sides of the bus were printed advertisements of various firms in Kalisz. So, of course, people wanted to know where we had been, so far from home, and where we were going. Mother talked to one of the group, telling them about the trip and also about our family and that she was looking for somebody from Kalisz, in the hope that they might have heard of or seen her husband.

"Oh," one man said, "my neighbor rented a room to a man from Kalisz."

"What is his name?" my mother asked.

"Stefan Zuker, he is an engineer."

"That is my dad!" I screamed, and Mother grew white as a sheet and began to tremble. I did not believe that it could be possible to find Father that way; perhaps the man did not know what he was talking about. But immediately he said that he was going to take us to him. We ran all the way, and it was not very nearby. We found him; there was no mistake. It was my father.

We had no time to ask questions, we just ran back to the bus, all three of us. Father told us all the details of his trips as soon as we were on the bus. He had waited until the last minute in Kalisz for his recruitment papers. They never came, and he had waited just a little too long. The Polish army dynamited the bridges when they left town and Father could not take his car. He took my bicycle—my beautiful, new gray two-wheeler that I loved so—put it on the boat, and that way got across the river. He had ridden it until he neared Warsaw and a soldier took it from him. It was too late to enter Warsaw so he walked on the back roads around the city toward Naleczow, but was too late there. He decided to go to Lublin and wait. He told us what we had already heard, that all the roads around Warsaw were like one big battlefield. He had been close to death many times. Once a bomb fell so near it killed two of his road companions and threw him across the road. Another time when the planes machine-gunned the people walking on the road, he jumped into the ditch and under a corpse that was lying there. That saved him. I hardly heard all these terrible stories. I held his hand all the way and thought I was dreaming. We have found Papa.

We arrived in Kalisz at midnight. The streets were empty. We did not know that the city was under martial law. That meant anybody walking the streets after 8 P.M. was shot on sight. The bus stopped on the corner of Pilsudski Street (the main street) and Wiejska. We lived in the third house from the corner. We took our belongings and walked home. We found our apartment as we had left it. My nurse Michasia, who had been with us since I was born, was home. She started to cry when she saw us. Her tears were of happiness and relief. She was so worried, not knowing where we were and what had happened to us. We were dirty and hungry, but we found everything we had been dreaming of—food, clean beds, soap, and water. My grandparents' apartment, across the hall, was in perfect order also.

The town had not suffered during the short war. The Germans took it without firing a shot. The streets looked different, though. They were full of German soldiers and "new Germans," the Volksdeutschen. They were Poles of German descent and had been given the option of becoming German citizens. On their arms they wore red bands with a black swastika and acted as though the world belonged to them. Red German flags flew from all the public buildings. It was so depressing. Grandfather Max came home after seeing it one time and did not go out again. He paced the room back and forth, talking to himself. I think he lost his mind.

After a few days Grandmother Maria (on Father's side) came home from Warsaw. She had lived through the siege of the capital and was glad to be home, but her apartment was already occupied. She had lived in one of the newest and nicest apartment buildings in the city and the Gestapo had taken over the whole block. She could not even get permission to enter her home and take a few of her belongings. She and her maid Marysia came to live with us. After a few days Grandmother Helena and Grandfather Max moved in with us as well. It was cheaper and supposedly safer.

My Aunt Lula and her mother returned home, but her husband did not. They heard he was somewhere on the Russian side. We heard the same about my cousin Berta and her brother Joe. Berta and her twin sister Lunia were very close to us. They had lost their parents when they were quite young and had grown up with my mother. They looked so much alike that nobody could tell them apart. But I always could tell which was which even when they dressed alike, as they very often did. Lunia had married my uncle Wladek (Father's brother) two years before and they lived somewhere in Central America. Wladek had lived there for many, many years. He had come home one summer, met Lunia, married her, and taken her back to America. Our family was small. It seems nobody wanted children. I was the only baby in the family and a little spoiled.

Days passed very slowly and in fear of the unknown. Every day the Germans published different laws, and every day they were more stringent with respect to how Jews were to behave. For example, when a man met a German in uniform on the street he had to take his hat off and step off the sidewalk. Later the same order was applied to Polish Christians.

My father began work as director of the office of the "Jewish Community." We were all worried because he had taken a job with so much responsibility. He could be put in jail or even shot for making the smallest mistake. More and more people disappeared into jails and were never heard from. If the community denied any of the Germans' demands, they took one hundred men as hostages, and killed every tenth one or fifth one—whatever the German in charge decided. Papa was a born optimist. He tried to see some good in everybody and everything. He thought that in that position, he would be able to help the family and learn all the news firsthand.

But every time he was late coming home, we thought we would never see him again. There was so much work that sometimes he stayed in the office the whole night. The Germans wanted lists of everything: how many Jews lived in town, all the properties owned by Jews, and how much they paid in taxes. One day the Gestapo commander did not like what the office personnel were doing, and they were all taken to the headquarters to wash the floors. Once finished, they were ordered to exercise all day, and those who were slow were beaten. Most of these men were elderly and not in good physical condition. They returned home with broken bones, black eyes, bruised all over. My father was one of the youngest in the group, a good sportsman, used to playing tennis and bicycle riding. He was not beaten physically, but morally he was crushed.

After having been treated like an animal, my father was no longer optimistic and good humored. He aged suddenly. He was quiet and somber and did not play games with me anymore. He still held me on his lap after dinner, just held me close. We did not speak, we just sat quietly. He was thinking about our bleak future and I was happy just to be close to him.

We lived in constant fear that they would come, they would take everything, they would separate us. The rumors were worse every day. In fact, they were not rumors. The worst came true in time.

The talk was that the western part of Poland, up to the river Warta, would be part of Germany, and the rest would be "Occupied Territory." The part that belonged to the Third Reich had to be cleaned up—free of Jews and Poles. Gestapo soldiers began to pick up people on the streets, load them in trucks, and send them to jails or concentration camps. Now women and children had to give way and step off the sidewalk when a soldier approached them.

At home we were slowly eating all our provisions, and waiting for tomorrow. Grandmother Maria started giving me lessons for a few hours every day from last year's books, so that I would not forget everything.

It was a cloudy autumn day in November 1939. I did not feel like getting up; I really did not have to. The schools were closed, there was no such thing as shopping—all the stores were closed anyway—and the bed was so warm.

It was about 10 A.M. when I got up and started to brush my hair. It took me a while to comb and braid it. It was almost to my waist and very thick. Suddenly in the mirror

I saw a German entering the front door, then another, and after him my father. They had come looking for some furniture they needed for their quarters. They needed living room furniture, a desk, some chairs and—who really knew what they wanted? Whatever struck their fancy one of them marked with a large piece of white chalk. When they had chosen what they wanted, they told everybody not to clean off the white numbers, or they would be shot. The Germans would pick everything up the next day.

We did not want to be home when they came, so Mama and I went to stay with my cousin, and Grandma Helena and Grandpa Max went for a walk. Grandmother Maria and the maids stayed home. We had not even taken off our coats at my cousin's house when one of her neighbors came in and told us that the Germans were evacuating Wiejska Street (our street), and running people out of their homes just as they were, without being able to take any of their belongings with them. They were taking everyone, under guard, to the monastery of Benedictine monks. Mama and I ran as fast as we could. Our home was third from the corner, surely one of the first to go. We got there too late. On the way we met a long column of people, under heavy guard, and we saw Father, Grandmother Maria, and the maids walking in the middle of hundreds of people. They could not talk to us and we could not talk to them. They were surrounded by German police, and people on the street could not stop even to look. They were pushed to move quickly and not look around. The Gestapo and SS men fired into the air constantly.

Our street was empty. The whole house was empty. They had left the janitor, and under penalty of death he was not supposed to let anybody in. We just stood there next to the big gate, not knowing what to do. My grandparents arrived, unaware of what had happened. We all went to my Aunt Lula's and there we stayed until evening. Mother went to the monastery and was able to talk to Papa. He was calm and hoped they would release him soon because he had some important keys from the office. That evening one of the maids,

Marysia, was able to escape and she told us what had happened.

One group of Germans had come and had taken what they wanted of the furniture, and right after them another group came. They rushed into all the apartments at the same time and started to eject everyone they found at home. The group that came to our apartment was the "bad" one. The officer in charge herded everybody into one room and searched them, one by one. Grandmother Maria had a small fruit knife in her purse. He became angry and accused her of concealing a murder weapon, saying that she wanted to kill Germans with it. How ridiculous, an old lady killing Germans with a paring knife. Papa had wanted to pick up his personal papers, and because of that he was struck across the face and his glasses fell and broke. Luckily he had an old spare pair on him. He could not see at all without glasses and it was impossible to buy a new pair. Our neighbor, the director of one of the best boys' schools in town, was beaten so badly, because he was carrying a hundred zloty, that he had to be carried downstairs.

The next day my father, Grandmother Maria, and my nurse were released. Because Father was working for the community they let him go home and pick up his papers. Marysia bribed the janitor, and got out of the apartment what she could. We all moved in with some friends that lived on the outskirts of town. We stayed there with twelve people in two small rooms for a few days and then decided to go to Warsaw. In the big city, we thought, it would be easier to survive. We could blend into the crowd.

chapter **3**

*W*e packed what was left of our fortune in knapsacks, and started our journey.

At the train station officials took all of us to "customs." In a way it was our fault because we piled all the knapsacks in one place and it looked suspicious to the patrolling German police. While the others were carrying the luggage to be inspected, Mother and I slowly moved away unnoticed. The train was coming, and it was only at the last minute that they let the rest of the family go. We were already on the train when we realized that one piece of luggage was missing. Mother gave the train attendant some money to look for it, and the train had started to move slowly away from the station when he threw it through the window. During the "inspection" the Germans had taken Grandmother Maria's opera glasses and two pairs of stockings. We had sewn all the money and some jewelry into our overcoats, inside the shoulder pads. The Germans did not find it. We were safe this time. We feared that they would search again on the train, but the trip was uneventful. We heard later that some of the cars were searched. The Germans knew that when people were leaving their homes, they took everything of value with them, and they were looking especially for money and jewelry.

We arrived in Warsaw about 9 P.M. and had to stay at the station all night because of the curfew. Mother fixed a little bed for me by putting two knapsacks together and covering me with a blanket. Everybody else just sat around close to each other to keep warm. They could not sleep, wondering what the next day would bring. We all had a little spark of hope that it would be better in Warsaw.

At about 4 A.M. a long cargo train arrived at the station. Nobody was there to unload it, so the Germans started to round up all the men who happened to be in the station and lined them up from the car to the warehouse and made them unload. One of the Germans, looking for more men, saw a bundle under the blanket, and thinking a man might be hiding there, screamed and pulled the blanket away. Awakened by his shouts, I opened my eyes and saw this terrible-looking face above me. He saw it was a child, threw the blanket back at me, and walked away still shouting.

At about 5 A.M. we left the station. The city was dark. A little snow was falling, and it was cold. It took us a while to straighten out our stiff legs and find some kind of transportation. Warsaw had suffered a lot during the siege. There were no streetcars or buses. The only way to get from one place to another was on wooden wagons that had rough wooden benches on the sides. Cars were only for the Germans. We were going to Chlodna Street, to some distant cousins that Grandmother Helena had always kept in touch with.

Aunt Pola had a large apartment in a big house that she owned. The apartment was bright, clean, and looked very comfortable. The first thing she did was to put me in her bed. Oh, it felt so wonderful. It was still warm. I slept until noon, when laughter awakened me. Aunt Pola was telling everybody a story: after taking care of everybody early this morning, she had gone back to bed. She was drowsy, half asleep, when she felt a hand on her face. She pushed it away, but it came back. Once, twice, then she felt a leg on her stomach. She jumped out of bed, trying to decide whether somebody strange was in her bed or it was a bad dream! And here on the pillow she saw a head full of curly brown hair and remembered that it was Lilly.

The next day we moved to our own place, or rather half our own. It was a four-bedroom apartment, and Mrs. Perow, the owner, let us have two bedrooms with kitchen privileges. It was on the fifth floor with no elevator, but it was convenient. Mrs. Perow lived there with her two daughters and grandson Josef. They were very nice to us and helped in every way they could.

The first few weeks in Warsaw passed quickly. To me everything was new and exciting. I went for long walks with Josef. He was a cute five-year-old and we got along well, though we did have our share of little quarrels.

In January some more of the family came to Warsaw from Lodz. There, as in Kalisz, life was becoming impossible. In the evenings we gathered at Aunt Pola's. The elders talked all the time, but for the children it was fun. I became friendly with three girls (very distant cousins), Janka, Krysia, and Erna. They were older than I, but they tolerated me, told me their secrets, and from time to time asked for little favors.

Winter that year was very cold and we did not have a supply of coal. Each room had a big tile stove. We started the fire late in the day, and let it die out early in the evening. Mother and Marysia went every day, looking for a small quantity of coal. It was very expensive. Marysia was like one of the family. She took care of Grandmother Maria and helped with all chores. My mama stayed in Kalisz. We just could not afford to take her with us.

That is how the winter of 1939–40 passed. In the spring Marysia went back to Kalisz to pick up some money that my grandmother had left there with friends. On the return trip she stopped in the little town of Koluszki. It was on the new border of the German Reich and the General Governorship (the new name for our old Poland). Her niece worked in Koluszki on a large farm taken from Polish owners and run by Germans. She gave Marysia some butter, cheese, eggs, and meat. We had a luxurious Easter dinner.

In the spring the Germans started what was called "swift search." They would run from house to house looking for ammunition and taking everything but that. Every day new and more stringent laws were announced. One of the worst was that all Jews ten years and older had to wear a white band with a blue Star of David on their left upper arm. After a few days they extended the law to all Jews. Even babies in carriages had to wear armbands. The penalty for not wearing them was concentration camp or death.

Then the hell started! The Germans made what they called "raids for the bands." They walked the streets with big rubber sticks and beat everyone they felt like, as long as they wore the white band. Now they were sure whom to hit and would not hit a German in civilian clothes by mistake. Gangs of youths ran the streets throwing stones through the windows of shops owned by Jews, which were required to have the Star of David posted in a visible place. Father and Grandfather did not go out. All the errands were done by Mother or Marysia. Marysia was an illiterate Polish country woman, and with her dark hair and long nose she looked more Jewish than Mother or me, but she did not have to wear the band.

Twice a week I went to my Aunt Irene's. She was giving me English lessons. Irene was my father's first cousin, a beautiful, tall, and extremely intelligent lady. She spoke many languages, and made her living by giving lessons. She lived a good distance from us, and without realizing the danger of my actions, I always took the white band off when I went to her house.

On one of those trips, going up Marszalkowska Street, I met a young man named Tad from Kalisz. I had been introduced to him and his family during one of our vacation trips. He was much older than I, tall and very handsome, and I really had a crush on him. When we passed each other on the street, he politely said hello without ever stopping, but every time I saw him my heart stopped beating and my legs started to shake.

My old friend Alik and his family lived in Warsaw now, and he came over almost every day. Alik was a year older than I, and thought he could manage me. In fact, he did whatever I wanted him to. I had him under my thumb. From the day I met Tad, I took Alik with me every chance I had, for long walks on Marszalkowska Street. We even went to the restaurant that we had heard Tad liked. When going to my lessons I always took the same route. I did meet him a few times, and every time he politely said hello. I was so in love that I lost my appetite. Finally Marysia—she knew all my secrets—told my mother and all hell broke loose. Mother explained to me how stupid the whole thing was and how dangerous. Tad could point me out to the police as a Jew without her armband. Walking on Marszalkowska Street was not safe either. The Germans picked young people from the streets and sent them to work camps in Germany. She forbade me to take that route again and she talked to me for a long time until I understood. It took me just a day or two to forget my great love. There were other things to think about.

At various points in the city, workers started to build walls. They closed off streets, and then somebody would change his mind and the wall would be torn down and another built two streets away. People started to talk about the "ghetto." I had no idea what it meant. I had never even heard the word. After a few weeks it became clear. They had walled in the part of the city where most of the Jewish population lived. It consisted of two sections, cut by Chlodna Street. They could not close in Chlodna because it was a main artery going east. In the beginning, part of Chlodna was included in what they called the Jewish quarter. To make it possible to walk from the northern part (much larger) to the southern part, a bridge was built high enough for the traffic below to flow freely. The traffic moved very fast so that no one could jump in or out of the buses. At first most people could pass in and out of the quarter with special permit cards. Many lived in one section and worked in the other. The checkpoints were at large streets with German SS soldiers guarding them.

Anybody who wanted to live in this so-called Jewish quarter could do so, but was automatically considered a Jew. Marysia did choose to stay with us, or rather with Grandmother Maria. She was very devoted to her, and in fact had nobody else to go to.

From that time on the Jews were not Poles anymore; just Jews. If you were born to parents of mixed religion, you were a Jew, and if even one of the grandparents was a Jew, the grandchild was a Jew.

All the Jews living outside the walls were forced to move in, and it became difficult to find a place to live. After looking for a long time, we rented one large room in the smaller, southern section on Krochmalna Street. Mrs. Novak, our landlady, gave us a sofa and a rollaway bed and we settled in. It was very cramped. We were squeezed together like sardines— seven in one room. I slept with my parents on the sofa, Max and Helena on the bed, Maria on the small love seat, and Marysia on the rollaway bed. We had a small two-burner gas stove outside the room to cook on.

The winter of 1940–41 was very severe. Our landlord had an ample supply of coal, so even hungry, we were warm. In general, living conditions were terrible and very expensive. People came into Warsaw from all the surrounding villages and small towns. They had no money, no relatives. They were forced to stay in what were called living quarters, but were really hell quarters. Each room was packed with as many as possible. Twice a day each person was given a bowl of watery soup and 300 grams of black bread. Shortly these houses were breeding places for typhoid and other infectious diseases. People became so weak that they just lay down on the sidewalks and died of hunger and cold.

Fewer and fewer entry permits were issued and those who obtained them were searched more and more thoroughly as they crossed the barriers.

Gradually merchants began to open a few stores, mostly food markets and coffee shops. There, for astronomical prices, we could buy pastry, white bread, even fruit, or have a dinner. Some people made fortunes smuggling food. They lived from day to day and spent fabulous sums on food and clothes. Everyone was required to have food cards, and we had to go out every day and wait in lines to buy what we needed. The lines grew ever longer.

Walking on the streets was like a nightmare. On every block there were corpses, sometimes covered with paper, other times half naked—someone had already stolen pieces of their clothing. At first I could not look at them. I would get off the sidewalk in order to pass them as far away as I could. As days passed everyone grew used to the sight, but I couldn't. It seemed that those frozen bodies always had their eyes open and nobody would come close enough to shut them. Most of the time, the family did not know what had happened to them, and many had no family. There was no such place as a morgue. Most of these corpses were taken by the garbage men—the streets had to be kept clean.

More and more people were robbed on the streets, especially for food. It happened to me once. I was coming home with a loaf of bread under my arm, when a young man ran up to me, grabbed the bread, bit off a big piece, and threw the rest back to me. Everything happened so fast that I did not have time to pick up the rest of the loaf; a group of small children grabbed it and ate it. I ran home, crying and shaking. Mother said I was white as a sheet. That was my last trip to the store by myself.

Father worked, without pay, for the committee to help people from Kalisz. Mother could not find work. I went to a small school where they taught us a little of everything, as well as how to sew. I really liked it. We could not get new materials, so we practiced on old garments. We ripped them apart and made something else out of the fabric. We also received lunch. I was happier there than at home.

Life at home was growing more and more nerve-wracking. Even the closest family cannot get along living seven in one room. There were small unimportant things—like someone not putting something away or somebody putting something away that should not have been put away—and there were larger misunderstandings.

Mother and her parents took care of their own food expenses and Grandmother Maria took care of me and Father. The head of this household was Marysia. She gave us two pieces of bread for breakfast and dinner and soup for lunch, usually some kind of barley or grits. From time to time Grandmother received packages from Switzerland with dry sausage, chocolate, and cheeses, but those things were off limits for us. Marysia kept them in a cupboard and from time to time gave us a piece. I did not pay much attention to that, but it hurt my mother very deeply. Sometimes when the soup was just impossible to eat, Mother would fix me some special noodles and Maggi broth, a real treat. One time, I shall never forget it, I took a piece of chocolate from the cupboard without asking and the next day Marysia put a padlock on those doors. It hurt me so much that I can still feel that piece of chocolate choking in my throat. Marysia did with my grandmother what she wanted and to keep peace Grandmother just agreed. Marysia would sit in the middle of the room and listen to everything everybody said. Mother could not stand her for what she was doing to my father and me and became very depressed. She lost weight and her hair started to turn white. We went out of the house just to be away from Marysia.

In August of 1940 Grandmother Helena had fallen ill with typhoid fever. We could not send her to the hospital; that was death for sure. Mother took care of her during the six weeks the illness lasted. The doctor came to see her every day. If the authorities found out that he had not sent a patient to the hospital, he would lose his license. He was very worried about complications. Grandma was weak, had high fever, and needed quiet rest, but with all the people in one room that was impossible. She lay in bed for fourteen days and the crisis passed. She slowly recovered. By the time she was well, Max had come down with the same disease. His was much worse. The day after the crisis passed, he developed hiccups that lasted for two days. Afterward the doctor said that if the hiccups had come the day before the crisis, he would have died. Grandmother Helena slowly gained strength and helped to take care of Max. She cooked, washed, and helped Mother take care of little chores. We were all amazed at her strength, because before the war she had had heart trouble. The doctors then did not let her even comb her hair—that could have been too much for her.

In November Mother found a job as cashier in a grocery store. During the fall it was not bad, but in the winter it was terrible. The store was not heated at all. She worked from eight in the morning to six in the evening and came home completely numb. Her hands and toes were frostbitten, she was exhausted physically and mentally. At home it was worse every day. Grandmother was selling the rest of her jewelry. To smuggle food into the ghetto was more and more difficult, and so food became more and more expensive. Mother knocked on every door looking for another job because she could not stand the cold. Now only people that worked could get food cards.

When we were home alone, which did not happen often, she talked to me about how I should behave, that whatever happened, I should be good to my family, respectful to the elders. She gave me all kinds of advice about what to do when she was gone. I could not imagine a life without my mother. She was everything that I had to live for. She gave me love and understanding, she cuddled me close to her heart and all my troubles melted away. I was an only child and I was spoiled. But my sheltered life was gone forever and now my mother was talking about leaving me alone.

I loved my father very much, but I could not get so close to him. He was very quiet, kept all his feeling inside. It hurt him deeply that he could not find work and had to depend on his mother for food, and everyone told him he was not pushy enough. His only hope was for a better tomorrow and to be able to live through this nightmare. That was everybody's wish. The worst pessimist in the family was Grandfather Max. He said over and over again that even when the Germans lost the war, they would kill everybody the day before.

chapter **4**

During the winter of 1941–42 it became increasingly difficult to buy food. Potatoes went up every day. We had to stay in line for hours to get some soup, and then when we got home we had nothing to warm it with. Hot or cold, the soup was inedible. It was full of wheat husk and rancid oats. A new dish was created: pancakes made from potato peelings. The skins were washed well, ground, and fried in some awful looking and smelling oil. I could not swallow them; I felt like the mess was growing in my mouth. I swallowed the first bite and tears came to my eyes; I just could not eat it. The only one who ate them and did not complain was my father.

The little gas stove we had for cooking became useless. Germans cut off the flow of gas to the ghetto. We tried to cook on the wood stove, but it hadn't been used for so long that it smoked badly and we just ate everything cold.

In February of 1942 I obtained a job in a factory that made glue and all sorts of ink. The factory was owned and operated by a Pole, Mr. Leszczynski, but all the production was for the army. It was located in the ghetto, and it employed about a hundred people from outside the ghetto, who had special passes and could go in and out freely. The factory needed more workmen and the Germans told them to get Jews. First the owner wanted to move the whole factory to so-called *aryjska strone* (Aryan zone), but it would have been too expensive, and the Germans did not want to give him more passes, so he took thirty people who lived in the ghetto and I was one of them. I was given the job because a friend of ours was the factory physician and knew the director well. I was a bit small and skinny and they took me on trial. After a week the director came and told me I could stay and that my work was very good. The pay was thirty-five zloty a week, and that was about enough to buy a loaf of bread, but there were many additional benefits. Every week I got a bag of groceries and every day a good, hot lunch.

I was very happy in my work; for eight hours I lived in a different world. I was well liked, the baby of the factory, and made friends who smuggled all sorts of little packages of food to me. They often shared their breakfast with me. These workers made fortunes by working in the ghetto. They smuggled food in and sold it for high prices; then bought clothes very cheaply, and sold them for high prices on the other side.

After working a month I received my first allotment and brought home flour, beans, a jar of marmalade, and some oil. The factory gave us all this from kitchen supplies. The Germans did not want to give us any extra food.

My work was not very hard. At first I was assigned to the ink department, pouring ink from the special container into hundreds of little bottles. I also put labels on the bottles —that was a much cleaner job. After a month they moved me upstairs—that was a promotion—and I did the same with glue. Then, even better, I had a little machine all to myself for closing tubes. Days passed quickly during this time. I was home by 5:30, a little tired, but happier.

In the meantime, Mother had also found a job in the office of statistics. It was part of the city, or rather ghetto, government. We went to work together and came home at about the same time. We were happy to work, and happy to be away from home and its tensions. At work we had to forget all our troubles, talk to people, and keep smiles on our faces, and that was not easy.

All the news we could obtain was from German papers and they proclaimed victory after victory on the Russian front. Someone, somewhere, had a secret radio, and from England they were telling people to try to survive—but how?

Food was more and more expensive, and the bodies of more people who had starved to death lay in the streets. Mother tried to give me the best morsels and the most nutritious food. She was worried that I would contract tuberculosis.

In May Father got a job. He was the happiest I had seen him since the war started. He was the only man in charge of the office in a small outlet of an ammunition factory that the Germans kept in the ghetto. The main factory of "Wilhelm Döring—Apparatenbau" was somewhere in Germany. How big and important this factory was we had no idea then. The place was small, on Komitetowa Street, and employed about twenty mechanics. They manufactured small parts for some unidentified machine.

And so the whole family was working and life was a little bit better, a little more normal.

I liked my work in the factory, but even though I did my work very well, I was not treated like the others. I could not complain about anything; I knew they could answer, "If you don't like it here, quit. We have hundreds who would like to work in your place." I could not complain to Mother, because she would want me to stop working, and I certainly did not want that to happen. So I kept quiet. I even enjoyed staying in lines for food, because I was with Mother; that was the time we could be together without Marysia listening to what we were talking about. We worked and brought the groceries home. All the cooking and housework fell on Grandmother Helena's shoulders. After her bout with typhoid, she regained her strength. Even though she was very thin, she said she felt well.

In July we felt a new wave of terror. The guards at the entrances to the ghetto were paid by the smugglers and turned their backs when sacks, usually of potatoes, flour, and sugar, were thrown over the walls, but now they became more difficult to bribe and started to shoot. Many smugglers were killed and further shootings were to discourage others from trying. The big "operators" were losing whole wagons, and even those who officially could go in, usually with coal, had to empty their wagons in the middle of the street so the guards could see if there was any food under the coal. SS men and Germans from the Ukraine had replaced German soldiers as guards.

Around the same time articles in the local papers discussed the "removal" of the ghetto from Warsaw, because it was a center of fast-spreading plague. The group of elders, the Committee, that governed the ghetto, tried everything possible. They had crews disinfect the houses, they tried to get all the sick to the hospitals, but this actually did not help much. The hunger, dirt, lack of medicines, and the conditions people lived in helped to spread disease. The hospitals were crowded two and three to a bed with the overflow lying on the floors. The Committee could do nothing about it.

chapter 5

On July 22, 1942, the order came: "Relocate" the Jews. The first to go were the people who had no means of support and were living in public quarters. If they went voluntarily they were to receive one kilogram of bread and one kilogram of marmalade per person. Many of these people actually went voluntarily, without knowing where they were being taken. They were instructed to assemble at the *Umschlagplatz*, where the trains were waiting to take them—where, nobody knew. Even the Jewish police did not know, and they were helping the German SS in this task.

They started to "clean" the streets. At first whoever had any document from work was safe. At home everybody was "covered." Father had received very good papers from the German firm, and he covered his mother. My mother covered her parents because Mother and I worked. That way everybody, supposedly, was safe. People envied us. We were saved.

The well-to-do tried to buy false papers or get their names on factory lists—very seldom successfully. The result was usually, "Ah, you work only on paper—get on the truck and go to the *Umschlagplatz*." The Jewish police had a daily quota and every day they were short. Then the Gestapo took over.

They blocked off street by street with machine guns, ran into each house, and shouted "OUT." People had to line up in the courtyard as they were with the papers in their hands. During the time everyone was outside, the Ukrainian soldiers ran into apartments, breaking doors, furniture, looking for people who might be hiding or sick in bed—these were killed on the spot.

Three days after the "action" started we were awakened by gunfire nearby. We froze: they were on our street. We had hardly enough time to dress before they ran into our courtyard. We were all white as sheets, and carried the papers downstairs in our hands. Even Father, who was always very calm, could not say a word. The Germans hated cowards, so even though we were terrified, we stood straight and just looked straight into their eyes. Sometimes when a man had good papers but was shaking from fear, they took him anyway.

That day we were allowed to go back home, but Father went directly from the courtyard to work. Later he told us that he was stopped many times and searched. He passed hundreds of people standing in the middle of the street surrounded by the Gestapo, ready to be delivered to the *Umschlagplatz*.

After a week the "action" worsened. They no longer honored papers for the families of workmen; only people who actually worked themselves were let go. They started to close small factories. People went to sleep thinking they had jobs, only to learn in the morning that they had none. They felt like the ground was sliding from under their feet. The "action" usually ended at 4 P.M. but as the week progressed it stretched until 6 P.M. People ran from place to place, expecting to find safety where the Germans had "cleaned" the day before, only to be caught when the Germans started from the same place again. Insanity.

At home everyone slept clothed, ready to go down in a minute. We each had our little bundle packed. The only food we had was what we received at work. The little bit that was left at home was for those who did not work. There were no more stores. All had been closed, robbed, or vandalized. More and more homes stood empty.

On the first of August Mr. Leszczynski did not let us go home. He gave us enough food for the whole day and told us that he would not be responsible for us outside the walls of the factory.

I was very frightened. I did not want to stay there, I wanted to go home and be with my family. I ran to the factory's doctor, who was a very good friend of the family, and I learned that his wife and daughter were in the factory as well. He talked to me for a long while, trying to explain why they were keeping us in. He said that all the streets around us were closed, that the Germans were "cleaning" the whole southern (small) ghetto. He called my father and he too had to stay in his office. Even the Polish workers were afraid to go out and stayed overnight. They put us all in the back of the building. If the Gestapo came in, they would see only the Polish workers, who had been kept in because of the shooting outside. It is difficult to express how we felt, locked in, not knowing what was happening to our families, listening to the shooting and screaming outside. That was the first such "action," but not the last. They took everybody they found in the homes, separated children from mothers, wives from husbands. The factory walls hid it all from our view, but we could hear the screams, the cries of the children, the crash of broken glass, shooting, the moans of the victims, and the roaring Germans. To this day I can't believe how humans can sound like that. It was more like the roar of bulls, and the laughs were worse than bestial.

After a while we ran to an upstairs corridor and tried

to look outside through a little narrow window. How long would it last? Below us we could see a little piece of the street, full of Germans running like wild animals and people standing in the middle, holding on to each other, and looking up we could see the cloudless blue sky of a summer day coming to an end. Was a God up there? If He was there, could He really see what was happening on earth? Why did He not send His miraculous thunder to clean it all?

At about seven in the evening the streets became quiet and the Polish workmen started to leave for home. Father called and said that everything at home was fine, the "action" had not gone that far. We stayed in the factory overnight. They gave us an empty barn to sleep in. It was clean and we slept on fresh hay. I had loved to play in the hay in the quiet countryside, listening to the birds chirping, looking at the strange shapes of the clouds, but now the hay was itchy. It felt like every little blade was pricking my skin, and I scratched and scratched.

The next day was warm and sunny, and we started to work as though nothing had happened the day before. At about four in the afternoon Mother came over and brought me my coat. She said I might need it to cover myself at night. She stayed only a very short time, saying that it was quiet outside, that she was tired and would go to bed early. She kissed me, and told me to take care of myself, to have courage. God willing, we would survive all this.

I embraced her, kissed her. My heart started to beat very fast, and my eyes filled with tears, but I did not want her to see it. I wanted her to stay with me. I needed her now, I wanted to have her near me forever.

I stayed at the gate until she disappeared around the corner—and that was the last time I saw my mother.

After she left, we heard movement on the streets. Germans marched in to continue the action in the small ghetto. We did not know which streets they were "cleaning," only that from far away we could hear shooting.

After about four hours it grew quiet.

We were sitting in the big dining hall when the doctor came in. His face was gray and his eyes were red. I did not have the courage to ask him for the news. I knew it was not good. He came to me to embrace me and told me that he did not want to lie to me: everybody at my home had been taken to the *Umschlagplatz*. Father had called and said he would try to get a German policeman from the factory and go there to free them. I felt like the earth had opened up in front of me. My head felt light and in that moment somebody picked me up and sat me on the bench. I was numb and could not comprehend what was happening. All the girls were standing around me but it was difficult for them to console me; it could happen to them in the next hour.

I could not cry, I felt so empty inside. The doctor tried to comfort me and told me over and over that Father worked for a very important firm and they would be able to help him.

I did not have much hope that Father would be able to save them. We knew days before it happened that the "action" was not for moving people to another place, but to send them to their death.

The Jewish police, who helped at the *Umschlagplatz*, told stories that were impossible to believe. Everybody knew now that they were going to be killed, but I don't think they knew how it would happen. Sometimes the freight cars were so full that people died from lack of air. Some transports went to the concentration camps, where they kept the young and able for work; others went to gas chambers. In other transports they covered the floors of the railroad cars with some poisonous powder which in the heat and moisture (everybody used the floor as a bathroom) produced gases that slowly killed the people.

I sat next to the phone throughout the night, hoping Father would call. Thousands of thoughts crossed my mind: that I would never see my mother again; that she had been here a few hours ago and now she was suffering somewhere, far from me, and I couldn't help her. Maybe she was already dead and I would never know where her grave was. A few hours ago she had been healthy, had talked to me, brought me my coat. Suddenly I remember all the screams, shooting, and moans of the wounded from the day before. Oh, God, I hope she is not wounded. And what happened to my grandmothers? Grandmother Maria had always said she would not let them take her alive. She had said she would slap a German and he would kill her for sure.

I thought about all this during the endless night. Early the next morning, Marysia came, her face red and puffy from crying. She was in a daze. I asked for permission to leave and together we ran home. On the way she told me all that had happened. Right after Mother had come home from seeing me, the "action" had started. They did not check any papers, but ran everybody into the streets and marched them to the *Umschlagplatz*. As they were passing an empty house with a little door that was half open, my mother pushed Marysia in and nobody noticed it. She ran to the basement and spent the whole night there. As she was running down the stairs she heard Mother's voice—"Save Lilly."

Marysia did not know how many hours she stayed down there, but when the morning came and it was very quiet, she ran home. Nobody was there. Then she ran to my father's office. He knew all about it and had hoped to save them, but in the morning it was too late; the trains had left during the night. The *Umschlagplatz* was empty, waiting for another "shipment."

We ran through the empty streets, hoping that we would find somebody home. Maybe somebody had been able to run away? It was so eerie, all the houses empty with broken windows, the doors creaking in the wind.

We finally ran into the backyard. I was the first to reach it, and I stopped. Broken furniture was scattered all over the yard. On the few trees that grew inside the courtyard, hung pieces of clothing, and in the middle of the yard was a large puddle of blood that we had to cross to get to our stairway. A terrible stench was all around us. Only the hope that I would find somebody at home made me cross this river of blood. I closed my eyes and jumped over it, disrupting a swarm of flies.

The apartment was in a shambles, with windows shattered, walls peppered with bullet holes, doors splintered. I sat down on the floor crying and started to pick up some pieces of clothing. Marysia stood next to me patting me on the head and saying, "Poor baby, poor baby, she is left alone in this world." That did not help at all; I just sat there and cried, cried until I had no more tears left and then just sat in the middle of that destruction not knowing what to do. We could not stay there because the German patrol could come anytime, and they would shoot on the spot.

Marysia raised me and led me out of the apartment. I just walked with her, like a zombie, not knowing where she was leading me, unable to see through my swollen eyelids. We went to my father. The place on Komitetowa Street was full of people. Everyone had brought their families to the factory. There were people everywhere, sitting on the stairs and around the yard on the little bundles they had saved. I looked around at all the women and children, and started to scream, "Where is my mother, why is she not here?"

Father took me in his arms and tried to explain to me that he had waited too long to go for them. He had wanted to leave them at home as long as possible; they were more comfortable there. The conditions in the factory were terrible. He had just waited too long.

That whole day I sat behind my father's desk and cried quietly so I would not disturb the men working nearby. Papa brought me some soup, but I could not swallow it. One of the girls who worked in the kitchen came to me and tried to feed me some black coffee and a piece of black bread, but the food would not pass my mouth.

I did not go to work that day and stayed with Papa that night. We put some blankets on the floor behind his desk and tried to sleep there. I could not close my eyes the whole night. Every time I tried, I saw my mother leaving me at work the day before and blood, blood everywhere.

The next day I went to work. I obtained papers from the Döring Company certifying that I lived in their buildings, and I also had papers from the Leszczynski Company certifying that I worked there. With those documents the sentry let me go through to work and back "home."

chapter 6

On the Döring factory grounds I met a girl who worked with me but lived there, because her mother worked for Döring. From then on Marta and I always walked to and from work together. It was so much better to have company walking through all the empty streets.

The small ghetto had been "cleaned" out. No one lived there and nobody was permitted to walk the streets there. The rumor was that after finishing all the Jews, the Germans would disinfect the whole section and let the Poles move in.

There were two big factories in this section of town. One was Döring and the other Tobens, which employed about three thousand people. These workers were given one street to live on. The street was completely sealed off, as was the Tobens factory. Tobens made uniforms for the army and employed a large number of women. To get to Döring's factory, workers were escorted by German soldiers to Komitetowa Street. Marta and I were the only two that worked at another factory and had to walk by ourselves. The militiamen looked at us in surprise and the soldiers usually smiled, and never searched us.

A few days later Marysia left. She took all her clothes and the last ten-dollar gold piece that Grandmother Maria had had and went to the other side of the walls. She wanted to look through all the things we had left, but Father did not let her. He hated her for all the troubles she had caused my mother, and the way she had treated him and his mother. Once she had even terrorized us with a threat of the Gestapo. She went to the Aryan zone and left no trace.

Father and I moved to a room we were given in one of the two houses that were occupied by Döring workers. The room was small and on the first floor. It would have been nice if we had been there alone, but we shared it with three men who worked with Papa.

There were two brothers, Natek and Henry, and the third man was Severyn. The latter was a young man whom I had met in the office the day I lost my mother. He worked at the desk next to Father's. He was always quiet, spoke to no one, and just worked.

The room was furnished with two sofas with a little table between them. Papa and I slept on one sofa, the brothers on the other, and Severyn had to move the table and sleep on the floor.

All the workers' families moved in one day. The narrow street was full of people running back and forth. The next day everybody had to go to work.

In September 1942 English planes started to bomb Warsaw. They came at night and tried to hit military objects. They were very well informed and one of their targets was Tobens. During all these raids we did not get out of bed. We were on the first floor and felt it would be silly to run just one floor down to the so-called shelter. First came the light, then the explosion. When I saw the light, I covered my head with the blanket so I would not hear the noise of the falling bombs. We were all very tired, working ten hours a day and not being able to sleep. After work I had to cook our dinner: soup. I did not complain. I was glad we had some potatoes and beans that Natek and Severyn scrounged from who knows where. Henry brought some bacon and we had delicious dinners and breakfasts. They all helped, but I was the chief cook. We were all one big family, bonded together by our circumstances.

One morning, after one of the longest raids, I went to sleep and did not wake up when the men left for work. I awakened with a terrible headache and decided to stay in bed the whole day. Dad, the last to leave, agreed that I should rest that day. At about seven, as usual, Marta came and was very surprised to see me in bed. I told her that I did not feel well and had decided to stay in bed, and would she please tell my boss. Marta was terrified at the thought of walking alone to work. She begged me, pleaded with me, got my clothes out and started to dress me. She looked so frightened that I dressed in a minute and we went.

All the way to work I kept telling her, "I am doing this just for you; if I get really sick, you will stay home and take care of me." We were a little late and walked very fast. After a while I was glad she had made me go.

The day in the factory went fairly smoothly. Just as we were leaving, one of the girls asked Marta and me if she could walk home with us. She had some family working for Tobens and wanted to see them. We said, "Sure, but we should not walk in a group, it is better to walk separately." She went through the gates a few steps ahead of us, and we kept the same distance walking the empty streets. Suddenly, from nowhere, came a German patrol. The girl in front of us panicked; she wanted to run to the next house, but the Germans saw her, called her, and told the militiaman to take her. He did not even check her documents.

Well, now it is our turn, I thought. Marta wanted to run also, but they had already seen us, so it was too late for that. I pinched Marta on the arm, and told her, "Let's just walk by." We held our heads high and walked straight by them. Nothing happened, so we continued walking, expecting every moment to be called back. We turned a corner and started to run, still thinking they would call us. We ran so fast I could not catch my breath; my mouth was dry, my tongue felt stiff. We did not slow down until we were almost at our street. We never saw our companion again.

When we entered our street it seemed strangely quiet. Usually at that time everybody was on the street, waiting for the working force to come home, to bring food. Kids—very few were left—ran to meet their fathers, and there was always a line waiting at the bread store.

We knew right away that something had happened. A few men were standing in front of each house, talking. When I neared our house I saw my father and he saw me in the same moment. He ran to me, embraced me very hard, and started to kiss me all over. He looked at me as though he was not sure it was me he was seeing.

That morning at about ten o'clock, the Germans had blocked off our street and taken everybody they found at home. The only women left at Döring were three girls who worked in the workshop, two in the kitchen, Marta and me.

Marta had saved me.

chapter 7

*D*uring the next few weeks they let us live.

I left my job at the factory. We could not walk there alone, we would have to have a German escort, but because the Leszczynski factory was owned by Poles, they could not employ or even be helped by German soldiers. Marta left her family and stayed at Leszczynski, but I did not want to leave Papa. After a few days and many talks with one of the directors of Döring, I obtained a job in the workshop operating a drill machine. I had never before seen this frightful-looking animal, but the work was not difficult. My job was to drill little holes in metal that was used for ammunition. The only thing we had to be very careful about was not to drill through the fingers.

At this time Döring began to expand the factory. They

took over the workshop that had formerly been the vocational school of the Jewish community and the buildings of the community itself. Döring brought over there all the machinery from the small workshops, reorganized the factory on Komitetowa Street, and made this place, on Grzybowska Street, part of the largest ammunition factory in occupied Poland.

Papa and I moved to Grzybowska Street. One building was the workshop, one had offices and drafting rooms, another was the kitchen. Father, an electrical engineer, received a new drawing board, and I received a new drill.

Natek and Severyn stayed on Komitetowa Street, but came often to see us and always brought a good supply of food. Komitetowa was in the Aryan zone now, and they smuggled whatever they could.

There were no living quarters for Jews on Grzybowska Street. They gave us a big hall and everybody slept where they could—on the tables, under the tables, on the chairs, and most of us on the floor.

Work went in two shifts, from 6 A.M to 6 P.M. and from 6 P.M. to 6 A.M. Father worked only the daytime shift; the offices were closed at night. We had one table to sleep on. When I worked the night shift that was fine, but when we both worked the day shift I slept on the floor. In a few days I became acquainted with my machine and easily made my quota of little holes in little bolts. There were only three girls working in this workshop, and all the men liked us and helped us as much as they could.

The Döring Company was one of the best factories to work for. We had to work very hard but we were treated like humans. In other places they sent people to the concentration camps or the ovens for even the smallest errors. We also had the best allotment of food, and because it was an ammunition factory it could stay in the Aryan zone.

It was not long before all this changed, however. The new order was for everybody to move to assigned houses in a small part of what had months before been the "large" ghetto. The ghetto, small or large, hardly existed any longer;

there were very few people left and they all worked for German industry. The new living quarters were walled in between Gesia, Muranowska, and Stawki streets. Döring people were given two houses. Some of the apartments were empty, some had a few pieces of broken furniture, but luckily the windows were not broken. Winter was coming. This whole part of the city was empty since all the Jews had been taken to the ovens. House by house, the Germans had carried off everything of value. They even tore open pillows, dug in basements, and demolished stoves looking for money and jewelry.

Döring gave us two big trucks and in one week everybody and everything was moved to these two houses. Father found a small but clean room for us on the fourth floor. Severyn arrived too late to get a room and did not want to live with strangers, so we took him in with us. Father was not very happy about it, but could not say no to him, and I liked the idea of having him around. Natek and Henry had a room just below us and we spent all our free time together.

Life was becoming so hard, so terribly sad, that we all thought: why should we suffer so much; sooner or later our time will come, why not go to the *Umschlagplatz* and let them take us, and end our misery? But the will to survive was stronger.

I got up at five o'clock every morning. While I warmed some coffee, Papa straightened the room a little, and at 6 A.M. we left the house. German guards took us in three groups, one to Komitetowa Street, one to Grzybowska Street, and one to Okopowa Street. It should have taken about an hour to get to work, but we often had to wait in line to pass the Gestapo post. There was only one way to leave the walled ghetto and one post. The guards checked papers and searched everybody. How long we had to wait depended on how thorough they were with the search. Sometimes it took ten minutes, sometimes an hour. The same thing happened twice a day. Whoever came home first started the fire and the cooking: soup every day.

I was so tired when I came home that all I wanted was

to go to bed, but I just could not let Papa and Severyn do all the work. It was becoming very cold. Severyn took care of our heating fuel. Every evening he went with a group of young men to look for wood or anything that could be burned. They took doors, window frames, steps, most of them already broken to pieces, from empty houses. Our little iron stove had one big advantage: it grew hot very fast. But the moment the fire died down the room was cold. In the morning the room was so cold that every time we opened our mouths steam came out, and thick ice formed on the windows. But we did not have time to shiver; we always rushed out to meet our group on time. They did not wait, and everyone was afraid to stay home.

Every so often I did not see Papa for a whole week. Papa always worked the day shift, while every second week I worked the night shift. During those days, we passed each other in the darkness of the morning and in the darkness of the evening somewhere on the streets. Sometimes we could recognize the group by the whistles the guards were using. When I worked the night shift, I went to bed at 6 A.M., slept until three in the afternoon, started the soup for Papa and Severyn, cleaned the room a little, and washed a few things. The six o'clock whistle was always too soon.

The few days each month when I had my period were the worst. In those times women used pieces of soft cloth and they had to be washed. I hated this job. And of course I had to do it when the men were not around. Every Sunday morning we had the big wash, and in the afternoon all the young people gathered in one room for tea and whatever somebody brought.

Father and I were very close but we never talked about the past. Life was so harsh and filled with work that we did not have time for serious talk and in fact we had no desire for it.

Severyn and I became very good friends. He tried to help us with all kinds of chores. Our friends thought we were in love, but the truth was that we were just friends and I loved him like a brother.

In these crazy times people were obsessed with getting married. Men who had lost their wives and children married women who had lost their husbands. Nobody knew how many days they had left and they tried to take advantage of every minute.

Eventually I realized that I missed Severyn when he was not around and my heart beat faster when I heard his steps near the door. He was very nice and very helpful, but distant.

I told my girl friend about my feelings, and she laughed and said, "You must be blind, everybody talks about you two being in love." I realized then that what I felt toward Severyn was more than just friendship.

My girl friend told me one day, "He is very young, he will change. When he is with me he always talks about you." I was just happy that we were together and he did not have any other girl friend. I felt so grown up, so mature, and I was happy to have good friends.

chapter 8

*J*n December of 1942 we lived through three "selections" in the factory. One of the worst Gestapo officers came to Warsaw to segregate all the Jews that were left and send the weak ones to the ovens. "Mr. Brown" sent them to the "sanitoriums" at Dachau, Majdanek, Birkenau, or Treblinka, to name a few. He stood in the middle of the courtyard with a rubber stick in his hand and pointed to the ones he wanted out of the line. Then the victim had to walk between two lines of soldiers to the wagons waiting in front of the gate. These men were not really German soldiers. They were the most vicious men on this earth—Germans from the Ukraine, trained to kill.

I was very quiet during these selections. I had decided what I was going to do. If "Mr. Brown" pointed the "magic wand" at my father, I was going with him.

Once he stopped near my father, turned to the director, and asked him something. The director probably told him that Father was needed, and he went away. Next to me was one of the girls who worked in the kitchen. She was very sure of herself because she lived with one of the German guards and thought she could do what she wanted. When one of the Gestapo was passing us she turned and smiled at him. The man slapped her on the face with his rubber club and said, "You see this club? Your brothers made it for us, so we can use it on you." He laughed and went away.

We went home that day even more depressed and worried about the future. The familiar empty streets looked emptier. Wind howled through the empty doorways and windows and blew up clouds of feathers. The streets were white, covered with the contents of torn pillows and comforters, with here and there broken dishes, torn clothes, and furniture—the fortunes of people who no longer existed. Sometimes a lonely cat ran across the street. I could see the shiny eyes and thought it might be the ghost of a person killed there, roaming the ruins, looking for a family.

At the checkpoint we had to wait longer than usual and the search was more thorough. Usually they let us take bread, but this time they took every piece they found.

At home we found a letter from a lady we did not know, telling us that my Aunt Lula had been taken during the last "selection" and if we wanted her clothes we could look for them in a certain place. Lula was the last of the family whom we had seen from time to time.

Until July of 1941 we had received packages and letters from my uncle—my father's brother—in Central America. After that we did not receive anything and we could not write. The ghetto was completely cut off from the world. Maybe we could have written a few words through someone who worked with Father, but it was too risky. The censorship was so strict that officials would come to the house and ask who the addressee was, if it was a relative. If they did not like the answers, the person who sent the letter could be accused of espionage. We understood how afraid people were to become involved in this.

We could not live only on the soup we received in the factory. Bit by bit we were selling what we could to buy a little food. Some people made money smuggling, but neither Papa nor I could do it. The few zloty we received from selling clothes went very fast. The last thing of any value we had was Papa's watch. He sold it and now had just a few pennies left.

Through Mr. Rucki, one of the engineers Papa worked with, we sent a note to Mr. Wendeski. He was a friend of my Grandmother Maria, and she had left all her silver with him. Father asked him if he could sell some of it and give the messenger the money.

After he had read the note, Mr. Wendeski was very disturbed; in fact, he was frightened. But then Mr. Rucki explained to him who he was, how he had received the note, that of our whole family only Stefan and Lilly were left and that we had no more money. He told Mr. Wendeski where we were working and how he could get in touch with us. Mr. Wendeski had reason to be afraid because he could have been shot for hiding Jewish belongings.

He told our messenger that Marysia, our Marysia, was working for his family and that she would be the one to help us. He called her in, and when he read her the note she burst into tears. She said she would come to the factory the next day, which was Sunday.

It was now January, and the Gestapo had begun "selections" in the living quarters, so Döring had kept us on the factory grounds again. We did not expect an answer to our note until Monday when Mr. Rucki came to work.

Living at the factory was terrible, but it was safer, and they gave us soup three times a day, so we did not have to worry about food. They did not tell us where to sleep. Everyone looked for his or her place. The office personnel took one drawing room and made a sleeping room out of it. Some slept on the tables, others tied blankets to the four legs for makeshift hammocks, which often deposited their occupants on the floor. Father had a table for us, but it was very uncomfortable. One of the girls, Maryla, had a straw mattress and shared it with me. She was alone, having lost her family in Lodz and somehow had come to Warsaw. There were ten people in this little room, but one more did not make much difference. Besides Maryla and me there were two married couples, another friend of ours, Danka, and her three brothers and sister-in-law. We slept in our clothes. In the morning we washed a little—water was scarce—first the women, then the men. We did try to keep the room clean. We feared lice and the other insects that breed in dirt. We took turns every day cleaning the room, washing the floor, and shaking all the blankets.

chapter **9**

$\mathcal{T}$he first of February, 1943, was Sunday, the day of rest. I got up early and went to the kitchen to make breakfast— soup—for all my roommates. I was just coming back with a big pot full of a mixture of water, barley, and a few carrots, when I heard Maryla calling me. "Hurry, hurry, somebody is waiting for you in the entry room!" She whispered in my ear, "Come right back and tell us who it is."

Someone was waiting for me in the little room; who could it be? I did not know a soul living outside. I knew a lot of people who had friends in Warsaw and they came to the factory, or sent packages. All they had to do was to give the guard at the gate five zloty and they could come and go any time. The factory was now in the middle of the Aryan zone. All the surrounding buildings were occupied by Poles and they could move freely in and out of the factory. But me—it must be a mistake. I gave the pot with soup to Maryla and ran to the gate.

The moment I walked into the room I was embraced by Marysia. I could not believe my eyes. How did she know where we were? Where had she come from? I did not even wait for her answer; I just took her by the hand and dragged her to our little room. Then she told me that after she had left us, she went to Mr. Wendeski and the Wendeskis had kept her there as a maid for their daughter and her family. Then yesterday Mr. Rucki had come and that was how she knew where we were. She brought us a great deal of food— bread, butter, and cooked meat. She said that was all she had brought because she was not sure if she would find us, but what she wanted to do was take me, little Lilly, with her to live—now.

Everybody looked at her startled and I just sat there with my mouth wide open. "But Marysia, how can you? It is impossible. We don't have a penny and I will not go without Papa."

Soon Papa came in. Someone had run to his office and told him what was going on. He was sincerely happy to see her. We both forgot the way she had behaved with the family, how much she had embittered our lives. Now she had come the moment she knew we needed her, and she seemed so sincere. The first thing she said when Papa came in was that she was going to take me with her. Papa smiled and said, "How do you imagine you can accomplish that?"

"Well," she said, "I know it is not easy. I have a place for Lilly in the same apartment house where I am working, at the shoemaker's. In a month I will quit this job and we will take a room together. I have some food saved and some money and that will do for some time. Later we will see."

"Marysia," I said, "that is out of the question; I have night shift this week. I have to go to work on Okopowa Street and the Döring people said they would let us go home this week. It seems everything is quiet in the ghetto."

"You are crazy! Tomorrow night I am coming to get you, and that is final," Marysia said. "I have to go now to cook dinner." She said good-bye to everybody and to me she said, "Remember, tomorrow evening, be ready."

After she left everybody was very quiet; then suddenly everybody started to talk: "You are lucky, what an opportunity, and you said you would think about it." "You know Mr. and Mrs. Gruszkiewicz, they have false papers and a lot of money and they cannot go because they have nobody they know and can trust to find a place to live," Maryla was telling me, all excited.

"I will not go without my father," I said very seriously. Now my father got into the conversation. He said it was a vital decision to make. We had a whole day to talk about all the pros and cons of my going with Marysia, and he was sure we would make the right decision.

After breakfast everybody went on their way, but I stayed in the room with Severyn. I wanted to have a heart-to-heart talk with him. I decided to tell him about all my feelings that I had kept inside for so long. I smiled, sat next to him, and told him that everybody thought it would be wonderful to leave this hell, but I was not so sure, because I did not want to leave my father and . . . him. It was very hard for me to say the last word, but I said it. The room was quiet; we could hear the voices of men debating outside.

Severyn got up and started to walk the floor, back and forth, back and forth. It seemed to me an hour but it probably took only a minute. Then he stopped in front of me, and in a very quiet and indifferent voice started to talk to me. "If you really have a chance to go away, you should, as fast as you can. Then you can look for a place to take your father. Give yourself—and him—a chance. I hope you are not deceiving yourself. You know for sure that our lives here are lost. One day more, maybe a week, and they will finish us the same way they finished our families. You are so young, your whole life is ahead of you, it would be unthinkable to throw this kind of opportunity away."

I wanted to scream, "Enough of this lecture, you idiot, don't you understand what I mean?" But I said in a quiet voice, "You're right, maybe after a while I will be able to get my father out." And I left the room, slamming the door behind me. I was angry. Angry because I had said too much. But after thinking about it for a while I realized there was little he could say. He wanted me to be free, free to start a new life.

I went to meet Papa. We did not have much time to talk. I had to be ready by 6 P.M. to start the night shift on Okopowa Street. From there we were supposed to go back to our house in the ghetto and return to the routine of an hour walk to and from work. It would be a whole week before I saw Papa again. We had to decide now!

Papa, after talking with some of his friends, had decided to let Marysia take me, and my opinion did not count. I was going and that was final. He talked to me for a long time, about what my life with Marysia could be. We both knew it would not be easy. He told me to be nice to her, to do whatever she wanted me to, and not to expect too much.

The whole factory knew I was going "out," and from their hearts they wished me the best.

I tried to persuade my father to wait one more week, arguing that maybe after one week Marysia would change her mind and not want me with her. Maybe after thinking about what could happen to her, she would not come for me. I just wanted to wait. But Father's decision was final, he wanted me to go as soon as possible—tomorrow. We never knew what the next hour might bring.

At 6 P.M. our group went to Okopowa Street. The next morning I was supposed to leave Okopowa, walk without the armband to Grzybowska Street, and wait there for Marysia. At work all we could talk about was my going "out." That was one night I did not feel tired, sleepy, or hungry.

In the early morning I talked to Maryla about how I should go to Grzybowska Street. I wanted to go out with all the Polish workers at 6 A.M. and spend the day with my father before leaving. It was dangerous; the whole section of town was deserted. It had been part of the small ghetto, recently given to the Polish and not yet fully occupied. At 6 A.M. it was deserted and patrolled by German soldiers.

Maryla tried to explain to me how dangerous it was, that I should go home and leave with the Grzybowska Street group in the evening. But I was very stubborn, I wanted to spend this whole day with Papa; we had so much to talk about. When she saw she could not change my mind, Maryla decided to go with me. She did not want me to go alone and I was very thankful.

I did not tell Severyn about my decision to leave that morning, but when we were washing our hands after work I turned to him and said, "Good-bye, Sev, I am leaving this morning. Be good."

"What are you talking about," he said. "We are going home together, we can say good-bye then."

"Not so," I said, "I am going with Maryla to Grzybowska Street this morning, and leaving from there this evening."

"You must be completely crazy to do it," he shouted. "Now that you have a chance to get out, you put yourself into that kind of dangerous situation."

"Well," I said, "maybe I am crazy, but since yesterday I have come to my senses about going out. Now that is decided. So, stay well, and I hope we will meet somewhere, sometime." And I left. Then I felt sorry. I knew Severyn was my sincere friend. Even though he seemed indifferent, he wanted the best for me. I was sorry I had been so rude, but it was too late to go back and ask forgiveness.

Before Maryla and I left we put our armbands in our pockets and then we walked out through the factory gate with some of the Polish girls.

After the bright lights of the halls in the factory, the streets were very dark. We had to stop for a moment to get used to the darkness and decide which way to go. As we walked the dark empty streets our hearts beat so hard we could feel them in our throats. We tried to avoid the more crowded streets. Finally we reached the corner of Wronia and Grzybowska. We still had a few more blocks to go to reach the factory when we heard the heavy steps, thump-thump, thump-thump, of the German patrol. I knew my face was white and I was shaking all over. Thank God it was dark and nobody could see our faces. We could hear the steps, closer and closer. They were so close that we could hear their conversation. Then they turned into Ciepla Street and we passed the corner and went straight to the factory. "Let's walk faster," I whispered to Maryla, and we almost ran to the gates. They were closed, and we rang the bell as hard as we could. From the other side of the street we heard again the thump-thump of the patrol closing in on us. Finally, after what we thought were hours, the gate opened and we ran in, slamming it hard behind us. The porter had let us in. Nothing bothered him and he never asked any questions.

The day passed quickly. I went around the factory to say good-bye to all the people I had worked with, gone through all the "selections" with, and sometimes had fun with. They were all good, very good friends, and in the last minutes I still wanted their opinion on what to do.

I was worried. I did not have the courage to go into the unknown, especially with Marysia as my benefactor. I did not have papers or money, I had to be hidden, but . . . where? I had to depend on her mercy, completely.

Papa and I talked about all this for hours, but his decision was final. I was going, but if I could not stand the conditions, he wanted me to come back.

At 5:30 Marysia came. She combed my hair very straight and put on my head a brown beret that she had brought. Everything so as to look just like anybody else. The last minute came suddenly. There was not much time to say good-bye, and everyone was nervous. The six o'clock bell rang and we walked out with the group of women workers.

The gate closed behind us. It was noisy, but I never noticed it. I could feel my heart pounding so loudly that I thought people near me must hear it.

That is how I started my new life, supposedly free, not behind the walls, but always with the same fear of death.

Now I could walk the streets of Warsaw just like all the other "Aryans." But I really did not have the right to do it, I was lying. I was pretending to be somebody I was not. I had not realized how nightmarish life like that could be. Everywhere I went, I felt that everybody I saw looked suspiciously at me. I lived in fear from that moment on. It was the second of February, 1943.

chapter 10

*W*alking with Marysia toward Dabrowski Plaza I was glad the streets were dark and nobody could see my face. On the way, Marysia told me where she had found a place for me to live and what I should say when we arrived. It would be best not to talk too much. I was going to stay at a shoemaker's apartment in the house where Marysia worked and lived. They were a very nice but poor family. They had one room and a kitchen for the man, his wife, and two children, Basia, eight years old, and Jasio, six years old. Marysia had told them that her niece had run away from a labor camp in Germany and she wanted Lilly to stay with them until she found a place for both of us. Meanwhile, Marysia thought these few days would be enough time to get me some false papers. I had to be registered in Warsaw and have a document like all the Poles living in the city. The Germans were continually checking papers everywhere.

It did not take us long to get to the street-level apartment. We rang the doorbell of what would be my first home in the Aryan zone.

The shoemaker's wife opened the door and let us in. She was a small, smiling woman and had been expecting me. Marysia had told her all kinds of stories and given her a lot of food in payment for my keep. The room was bright and clean, the children were cute and, as children are, very curious. Marysia left me there. She had to go to prepare dinner for her employers.

I was alone and did not know what to do.

The children took me by my hands, sat me on the sofa, and started asking questions—where I had come from, where was the luggage—but their mother sent them to bed, telling them I was tired from the trip. She prepared the sofa for me to sleep on. I was very grateful to her and went right to bed and pretended I had gone to sleep.

I wanted to cry. My body shook but no sound came out: I couldn't let it. I covered my head with the blanket, stuffed a handkerchief into my mouth, and after a while went to sleep.

I ate meals with the family and helped them to clean. They were very happy with all the staples Marysia had given them. The poor people did not know what price they could pay for all this. One big problem with this place was that people came in and out all day long to bring or pick up shoes. It was not safe for me to be seen by many strangers. Every time somebody walked in I tried to be busy with something and turn my back to them or read stories to the children. It was just too risky to stay there for any length of time.

After two days Marysia got in touch with Mrs. Kazia Lewicka. She was also from Kalisz, and had known my whole family and me when I was a little girl. She had moved to Warsaw a long time before the war.

(Kazia in time became my best friend, somebody I could

trust without asking any questions. I could put my life in her hands without hesitation. She is as good, just, and courageous a woman as I have ever met. She is still living in Warsaw and I hope to see her one day if it is humanly possible.)

At about 6 P.M., the safest hour, Marysia and Kazia came for me. We went to the little park nearby to talk and decide what to do. It was completely dark outside and we could speak freely. Kazia knew a woman who lived in the Mokotow section of town. She worked all day and had nobody to leave her baby with. Kazia thought it would be ideal for me to take care of the little boy in exchange for a place to sleep. We went there the next evening. The place was a terrible-looking dump, a long building, narrow, with paint peeling. It had seven one-room apartments, and on the side stood a nice small house where the owner lived and had his office.

Kazia told the lady the same story again—that Marysia was my aunt, that I had run away from a labor camp in Germany and had no identification papers as yet, and that my aunt was working and would only come to sleep.

The woman agreed to have us and was happy that she could go to work and be sure that her son was being taken care of. The next day we moved to Stasia's place.

I had orders not to open the door and never go out. If somebody knocked on the door I had to stay quiet and pretend nobody was home. It was frightening.

Marysia arrived every evening with my supper. During the day I cooked some soup for myself and the baby. At night we put a straw mattress on the floor and slept there. The room was damp and cold, and we had only enough wood to keep a little fire burning during the day. Stasia was happy that we were there. Marysia brought her bags of flour, sugar, barley—things she could not afford to buy. The baby was happier because he had somebody with him all the time and was fed and cleaned, and I was glad to have things to do.

Two weeks passed. Kazia came almost every day. She lived nearby and stopped on her way to work.

One evening Marysia burst in, white and shaken. She

said that on her way home the landlord had stopped her and told her that he wanted to see both of us in his office. She said, "Nothing good will come of this." I put my coat on and we went downstairs.

The landlord waited for us behind a huge old desk. He was about forty with a very long but nice face and a sincere smile. When I looked at him I knew he would do us no harm.

He did not waste time on small talk, but came right to the point. He said that Mr. Dymski, Kazia's husband, had come to him and told him that Marysia was hiding a Jewish girl, that she had money, and that he, the landlord, should get the money and split it with Dymski and then run us out.

I felt weak and my head started to spin. I thought it was the end. The man kept talking. He said he would not do such a thing, but we should know what kind of man Mr. Dymski was and leave this place immediately without a trace. He said Dymski would not wait long and if he realized that he, the landlord, was doing nothing, he might look for somebody else to blackmail us or go to the Gestapo. He promised to hold Dymski in suspense for a day or two and then tell him that we had left and he did not know where we had gone.

He was one of the very few people who did not jump at the idea of taking money from people who had no way out. We thanked him again and again and told him that by the next morning we would be gone.

We walked out not knowing where to go. It was very cold and windy; the snow squeaked under our boots, but I was so hot that sweat dripped from my nose. We did not have much time; it was 8 P.M. Nobody could be on the streets. Our only hope was Kazia, but what would happen if her mate was home? We took a chance. Marysia went first; the apartment was on the second floor. I waited downstairs. Luck was with us; he was not there.

chapter 11

*K*azia opened the door, and when she saw Marysia, white and wide-eyed, she became frightened. With Kazia in the room was her younger brother Anek. They called me upstairs and started to ask us a million questions. I did not open my mouth. Marysia told them everything and then said, "What are we going to do, where shall we go?"

Kazia was furious. "I had not dreamed he could stoop that low," she said. "He always was an SOB, but I did not think he could do such a thing. Well, I certainly messed you up. Now we will have to straighten it out, right Anek?" She looked at her brother. Meanwhile he was observing me. I had felt it the whole time Kazia and Marysia were talking. I must have looked terrible—pale, skinny, with my hair parted in the middle and combed very straight. The only good feature was my eyes and now they were filled with tears. I really did not want to cry, but the tears were dropping on my gloves. I had never thought to take them off.

"There's no other way," said Anek. "Kazia, you take Lilly to Rakowiecka Street. I will go with Marysia to get their things. Don't say a word to Dymski or anybody else."

It took about ten minutes to walk from Kazia's place to Rakowiecka Street. On the way Kazia told me all about the place. It was a small brick building, with a glue factory on the first floor. On the second floor the janitor and his wife lived in a two-room apartment, and Anek kept one room across the hall. Mr. and Mrs. Wojciech were in their late seventies. They cleaned the factory and took care of a good-sized garden, about an acre, in the back. They grew all kinds of vegetables for their own use and gave part of their produce to Miss Wanda, the owner of the factory. On one side of the garden there were a few smaller buildings, in one of which Anek was raising rabbits and pigeons.

Wanda was Polish, but had some German blood and had become a German citizen, a despised *Volksdeutsche*. On paper she was the sole owner of the factory, buildings, and land, but in reality she split the profits with Anek's brother, Jan. The business was Jan's idea, but as a Pole he could not own a factory that produced war materials. They had opened the factory to produce glue used by the Germans to mix with paint for war machinery. It was a wonderful business and they made a great deal of money. The Germans gave them all the raw materials and most of the glue went on the free market. That was where the money was coming from.

Anek worked there and Kazia worked for Wanda as her housekeeper. Anek lived with his brother and his brother's wife, Olga, but had a room in the factory as a convenience. Anek had been in the Polish army in the 1939 war and had been taken prisoner. A year later he had been released and started to work in the factory. He was not a partner but made good money and spent most of it. He was a happy-go-lucky bachelor and that kind of life was expensive anytime, in war or peace.

Suddenly Kazia stopped. We were there and soon Marysia and Anek arrived. Anek walked in first and told the old couple that Marysia was his cousin and I her niece, that we had no place to live, and that he knew they would not mind having us for a while. They would do anything for him; they loved him like a son.

The apartment was clean and warm. We entered a large room, their bedroom, living room, and dining room combined. The second room was smaller and served as the kitchen. That is where they let us stay. Anek scrounged a bed from somewhere. We had a table and two chairs and could use the stove when we needed it. They had plenty of wood, so heating was not a problem. Marysia gave them all our provisions. They gave me lunches, but we cooked our own dinners. Marysia still worked, but she had to leave before the office downstairs opened and had to come back after everyone was gone.

This place was ideal. There were no neighbors to snoop around, it was clean and warm, and the people were good and trusting.

After a few weeks Marysia stopped working. Mr. Wendeski was afraid that if the Germans caught me, he might be in trouble. Marysia sold the silver he had kept, so we had some money. We did not pay rent. Anek was giving Mrs. Wojciech all sorts of gifts—mainly staples—and they were happy with this arrangement. Kazia and Anek helped us as much as they could, but the greatest help was the roof over our heads. Marysia could not have done it alone.

During the day I stayed in the room, but at dusk Anek took me for a walk in the garden. If he was not home I often sneaked out alone and walked close to the trees so that nobody could see me. The factory and the garden were surrounded by a high fence, but people from the tall buildings on one side could still see down into the garden.

Spring was coming, the most beautiful time of the year.

The garden began to look so different; the fruit trees started to bloom, and flowers were everywhere. Mrs. Wojciech began to prepare the earth for planting her vegetables. She was so busy outside that all the work inside was left to me. Kazia had her vegetable garden in front of the factory. Every day after work she came and worked in it. During the war every piece of ground was utilized in some way and the government encouraged people to grow vegetables rather than flowers. Kazia used the largest part of the plot for potatoes, but she also had some carrots, beans, and beets, and next to the wall she planted tomatoes.

From my window I could see a long line of bushes on one side of the garden. I had not known what they were, but now I recognized them—they were lilacs, my favorite flowers. Every day the buds grew bigger and bigger until finally they were all in bloom. I could sit next to the window and almost touch them and in the early evening the room was filled with their fragrance.

Once a week, Marysia went to Grzybowska Street and took whatever we had to Papa—bread, butter, and some cooked meals. I wrote him long letters and he answered every week. After every visit I felt better and I was more hopeful that we would both survive.

I talked to Anek about trying to get Papa out, but it was so much more difficult to hide a man, and we did not have enough money to buy false papers. Papa's letters were hopeful. He said they were working hard but the Germans were letting them alone.

Spring was here in all her glory. Everybody worked in the garden to finish planting. At one end of the garden was an empty shed and Anek's brother, Jan, decided to start a rabbit farm. Not just any kind of rabbits. He bought a pair of white angora, a pair of white with black spots, and a pair of bluish-grays. They were beautiful and a special breed. The workmen built cages by the dozens and put them all into one shed. After a short time the cages were full of little rabbits. They were so cute. The angoras needed a lot of care; they had to be combed and the wool saved. Every evening I helped Anek to comb them, feed them, and change the water. I was spending more and more time with Anek. He hardly ever went to his brother's house. He ate with us more often and Marysia did not like it at all. She could not say much, because he was helping us; because of him we had a safe place to live. She told me every day how thankful I should be that she had taken me with her (I really was), and how she had run the risk of being killed (that was true). She told me how grateful I should be again and again. I think she was sorry sometimes that she had taken me; the burden was overpowering. She counted on Kazia and Anek for help if anything should go wrong, but she wanted all the glory for herself.

There were moments when I wanted to go back, but back where? One day, toward the middle of April, Marysia went to see Papa with the usual package and returned home with it. There had been nobody to leave it for. A few days earlier Döring had closed the Grzybowska Street factory and all the workmen had been taken to the concentration camps.

I was not supposed to cry during the day. The good old people might suspect something. I had to wait until night. I lay in bed with my eyes wide open; my head felt empty and I could not cry. Now I was all alone in this terrible world. Why should I live, why should I stay in this Aryan zone, hiding, endangering all these people? But I did not have enough courage to walk out on the street and tell the first policeman who I was.

The next morning Anek came with the news that the last Jews in the ghetto had started to fight the Germans. They had arms but there were too few left to do any good. But they did fight, and miraculously held out with small arms against German tanks and artillery for several weeks. At least they had the satisfaction that they had died fighting. The Germans then burned what was left of the houses. They must have known that something was going to happen, because a few days earlier they had closed all the outposts outside the ghetto. That is what had happened to Döring and my father. They took them—nobody knew where—just as months before they had taken my mother and the rest of my family and all the other families. I will never find their graves; they were burned in the ovens in the concentration camps and their ashes were thrown in the wind . . . and I will never know how they suffered before their deaths.

chapter 12

*A*nek tried to console me as best he could. It made no difference. I was not interested in what was going on around me. I did not hide my feelings. I did not talk much and did not care if Mr. and Mrs. Wojciech suspected something. The poor people thought I was sick and tried to give me the best morsels. Mr. Wojciech brought me fresh flowers from the garden every day—the most beautiful, fresh-smelling lilacs. I love lilacs; they are a symbol of Polish spring. I sat for hours and looked for the little blossom with five petals. Polish legend says it brings good luck if you find one. But what kind of good luck could I expect?

Marysia and Anek tried to get me identification papers, but it was not easy. During that time the Germans issued an order that all Poles must have new identification papers, called *Kennkarte*. Everyone had to go in person to an assigned place with a birth certificate, two pictures, and a registration slip that proved that you lived at your address.

Marysia obtained a birth certificate for me, through somebody she knew. Anek supplied the registration slip, and they decided it would be better if I went for the *Kennkarte*. It would be a genuine document that could be checked. The Germans searched homes and businesses all the time and that kind of document was safe. Also, they could check it at the registration office and the copy was there.

My new name was Stefania Bujanowska and I was now to be twenty years old. Poor Stefania had died a long time ago and they had been able to buy her birth certificate for me. I had to take all these papers to the assigned office. I was terrified. It was the first time I had walked on the streets of Warsaw in the daytime. I was dressed very plainly, just like a country girl. But everything went well, and I was to return in a week to pick up the *Kennkarte*.

A week later I went to pick up my papers, but the man in the office said that they had to check something more and to come next week. I did not go there again; it was too risky to go the third time. We did not know how, but Anek obtained a *Kennkarte* for me with the same name. The only difference between this one and the one I would have received from the office was that it was not registered in the city files or German files. But it was good enough to use on the street or if there was a house search. If somebody denounced me, no papers would be good enough.

Later we found out how Anek had obtained this paper for me. He was an active member of the underground organization AK (*Armja Krajowa*—Polish Army). They had people who specialized in false papers. They needed them for their own members, who often had to change names.

The summer came. The garden looked beautiful, the blossoms on the fruit trees were gone and little apples and pears started to appear. My favorite pastimes were looking at the garden and walking with Anek under the trees in the evening or helping him to feed the rabbits.

One day as we were walking slowly, talking about everything and nothing, Anek stopped. His face was very serious; he embraced me and started to kiss my eyes, cheeks, and lips. At first I was stunned. Then I realized I was happy to be so near him and have his arms around me. He kissed me so gently and then held my face in his hands so that I could look straight into his eyes. He started to talk, very slowly. It seemed as though he was weighing every word.

He said that he did not want me to think he was taking advantage of the situation and he did not want my gratitude to influence my answer. He said that he had fallen in love with me the moment he saw me at Kazia's apartment. He knew how much I had gone through in my young life, that the last year had been a terrible nightmare, but life had to go on and if we both survived this war, he wanted to marry me. He did not want my answer now, he wanted to wait until the war was over for me to make up my mind. I was stunned and could not open my mouth to say a word. All I could think about was what Marysia was always telling me, that Anek was doing all this for us because of her. She had been his family friend for many years, she and Kazia were like sisters. I could only think, "She was wrong, Anek loves me, and that is why he is doing it."

That night I told Marysia everything and she was irate. She told me that Anek wanted to marry me because I had a rich uncle in America who would send him money or take us to live there. She said that now, during the war, Anek was making money and being a big shot, but after the war when everything returned to normal he would just be a shoemaker, as he had been before the war.

If only I could have run from the room and all her nagging, or could have stuffed something in her mouth. I answered her in a very quiet voice. "I think you are the one who is waiting for all this money from America; otherwise how could you think about it? You hate Anek because you are afraid that all my gratitude will go to him. How do you know whether we will survive this war? How do you know that my uncle will send money? Don't count on it. Maybe Anek will have to make shoes to support us. What you say is dirty; you just want everything for yourself. You know perfectly well that without Anek and Kazia's help, you could not keep me here, and you were ready one time to send me back to Papa."

She knew that all I had said was true, so she turned away from me in bed without answering.

I had never remotely imagined that I could be happy again. I had asked God to take me with the ones I loved, because I did not think I could live without them, but now God had sent me Anek.

chapter 13

*U*ntil July everything was quiet in the little glue factory. It became more and more dangerous to walk in the streets. The Germans had finished with the Jews and now they started with the Poles. They captured men and women on the streets and sent them to work in the fields in Germany. More and more Poles joined underground organizations, of which the most powerful was AK. They held secret meetings, organized attacks on high-ranking German officers, and killed Poles that worked for the Gestapo. They ran guerrilla training centers for young boys and men. Each new member had to be sponsored by two old members who would vouch for him and take responsibility for whatever he did. Each small group had a commander, but they did not know each other's names; they were known only by pseudonyms.

Anek as an ex-soldier was very active in this organization and so in greater danger. The Germans tried very hard to prevent Poles from organizing. They had spies everywhere and we heard daily of mass arrests and shootings. Many good patriots were rotting in jails, being tortured to reveal the names of their comrades.

In the first days of July 1943 Marysia saw Mr. Dymski not far from the factory. She was quite sure that he had seen her. The next day Kazia came over; she was furious. She said that Dymski had told her that that woman and the girl must be hiding in the factory because he had seen Marysia around a few times.

Now that he suspected where I was, the place was no longer safe, not for me and not for the people around me. I had to run again. But where?

Anek had a good friend who was in his unit in the AK, and he hoped that Zygmunt would take me. He went there right away and the next evening I moved.

Zygmunt and his wife lived in the center of the city in a two-room apartment with a kitchen. They slept in the living room and gave me a small room in the back. Marysia stayed at the factory. Kazia told Dymski that Marysia was living there but that they had sent me somewhere in the country.

Zygmunt and his wife, whom he affectionately called Cipka, were really an odd couple. He was an artist, a painter —not too good a one, I think. He made a living by buying and selling whatever he could. He was a very handsome and debonair man and she was much older and quite ugly. She cooked, washed, cleaned house, and stayed home most of the time. He was hardly ever home.

Zygmunt loved Anek like a younger brother. They respected each other and were bonded by the danger of working together in AK.

When he agreed to take me in, Zygmunt told me what I could and could not do. Nobody was to know that I lived there. He did not want me to open the door, and if anybody came to visit them I must stay in the back room and be quiet.

I could not sit near windows where I might be visible to the neighbors. It was not too bad, except that from time to time one of their neighbors came to visit, and she stayed for hours. When she came in the evening I had to stay in the dark. Nobody would leave a light burning in an "empty" room.

Once a month the organization had a meeting at Zygmunt's house. When it was over, Anek, Zygmunt, and the commander of the group stayed, had a glass of wine, and talked some more about the strategy of their next move.

Their commander, Mr. X—nobody knew his name—was a very distinguished-looking man. He looked like he belonged to the Polish nobility, and he probably did. He was the one who had gotten me the *Kennkarte*, and after a month he said he could put me on the list of inactive AK members. In time I might be of help. I do not know if he actually ever put my name on this list.

One of those evenings in September of 1943, when we were all sitting around the table, Anek told Mr. X that he would like to marry me, though it would be better to wait until the war was over. But, he said, who knew how long that would be.

"Well," Mr. X said, "it would be best to get married legally in the church, but priests must write a detailed report for the German authorities about every wedding or christening, and the Germans look for discrepancies. That would be too risky.

"But," Mr. X said again, "we can get our field chaplain, and with me and Zyga [that was Zygmunt's pseudonym] as witnesses, the marriage will be legal in the eyes of God and the Free Polish Government. After the war, all the papers will automatically be registered."

One week later we were married. Our marriage vows were blessed by the field chaplain and witnessed by Zygmunt and Mr. X as a representative of the Free Polish Government. There was a third man present, whom I had never met before, who registered everything in the secret files.

The next morning Marysia came and started to tell me

stories about Anek. She told me that he had not come home the night before, that he probably had met some new girl friend, was bored with me, and was starting to run around. She tried to discredit Anek in my eyes, to tell me that everything he did was strictly business and not because he had any feelings for me. It was very hard to take. I had no way to check all her gossip, but I knew that she was lying to me. I knew Anek loved me. He was risking his life and his friends to help me now.

After her long speech I told her that I knew Anek had not come home last night because we were married.

I thought she was going to faint. Her eyes grew large and round like saucers, and then she became enraged. She started to scream, "So that is what you are doing behind my back. I knew sooner or later you would end like that. That SOB will do anything to his advantage—but you, you are not a saint—you let it happen."

"I am not a saint," I said, "and Anek is not an SOB, and in the future bite your tongue before you say something bad about him. I love him and I want to be with him, and I don't see a thing wrong with it."

She did not answer me. Instead, she turned around and ran out, slamming the door behind her. She was not angry for long. Two days later she came back and we never mentioned our conversation.

Day after day I sat in the little room knitting sweaters and reading. Marysia came every day and frankly I was not too happy to see her so often. Kazia came after work for a few minutes. Anek came home soon after five, but when he was a little late I worried and thought that something terrible had happened to him. He often had work to do for AK, but he never told me what it was or where. Sometimes the Germans stopped the streetcars to check papers, and that took an hour or so. Sometimes he did tell me where AK had sent him and what he had done, but always after the fact.

The summer had been hot, with very little rain. Autumn came and I did not go outside at all. The tall buildings around ours made the room dark even on a sunny day. I had not felt the warmth of sunshine since I had moved to this place. Twice Anek took me for a walk around the block to get a whiff of fresh air, but always at dusk.

Autumn came and with it cold winds and rains. We did not have enough coal to heat every room. Cipka kept a fire going in the kitchen. It kept that room warm and at the same time we could have hot meals. But when somebody knocked at the door I had to go to my room, and it was cold there. Sometimes whoever came stayed for hours and I was so cold all I could do was go to bed and pull all the covers over me.

A few weeks before Christmas 1943 Anek decided to take me back to live in the factory. It was safer there. In town the Germans took young people from the streets and from buildings for forced labor. We talked about it with Kazia, and the only thing that held us back was Dymski. It was becoming more and more difficult for Anek to supply Zygmunt with food, and now that winter was growing bitter cold, with wood and coal.

Finally he decided to have a little talk with Mr. Dymski. The situation was peculiar. Kazia worked for AK with her brothers, and the man she lived with was ready to denounce anything or anybody to the Germans for money.

Anek went to his place and told him clearly, "I am taking Lilly to live in the factory. If you open your mouth to anybody about it, you are signing your own death warrant." Dymski knew very well that the AK was growing more and more powerful. Every day they killed Poles who collaborated with the Germans. He knew that Anek's threat was not idle.

Kazia had known that Anek was going to talk to Dymski that day, but when she came home he did not say a word about it. Poor Kazia lived under the same roof with this beast of a man. They had no sympathy with one another, but under the circumstances could not live apart. Life was very harsh for Kazia. She was a mother figure for her younger brother and sisters, but for her older brother, Jan, she was not good enough. She did not dress well enough or drink enough.

Kazia had a younger sister, Rita, who had two small children and a husband in a German labor camp. Kazia fed and clothed them throughout the war. Had it not been for her and Anek's help, they would not have survived. I had never met Rita, but I was hoping to after the war. She lived in Praga, on the other side of the river. The river Wisla cut the city into two parts—on the east, Praga, on the west, Warsaw. I did not know then that I would meet Rita and her children long before the end of the war.

chapter 14

At the end of November I returned to live in the factory. Anek arranged his little room to be more comfortable for both of us. He put in a small iron stove to cook on and it gave off so much heat that I could walk around in short sleeves.

Jan did not want me in the factory. He was afraid that Wanda might find out and he feared for his own safety as well. Anek told him to behave like he did not know a thing. As far as Wanda was concerned, she was afraid for her own reasons. The news from the German fronts was bad, and she was trying to be extra nice to her Polish "friends."

Eventually Wanda learned that somebody was living with Anek upstairs, but she never saw me. She told him a few times that she wanted to meet the girl, but Anek told her, "In time, in time."

Dymski kept his mouth shut, Christmas was around the corner, and everything seemed to be going well. Snow started to fall, and frost painted beautiful pictures on the windows. It was very cold outside but my little room was warm and cozy.

Anek had to get up early to open the factory. At about eight o'clock he came for breakfast. For lunch we usually had some soup. We ate a lot of beans, all kinds of beans. Twice a week we had some meat. I saved some flour and fat for Christmas cakes. The day before Christmas Eve Marysia baked some poppy seed cakes that turned out beautifully. We made a big bowl of noodles with poppy seeds (which we ate for days after Christmas), and we had sauerkraut, beans, and some cooked fruit. It was a meal fit for a king. Marysia, Kazia, and her cousin Elki came for dinner. We even had some vodka to cheer the holidays. There was no midnight Mass—everybody had to be off the streets by 8 P.M.—but it was the custom to share a piece of altar bread and wish each other all the best. After we had done that, everybody left. Anek and I sat next to our little Christmas tree and shared some more of the holy bread and wished for a better tomorrow.

Christmas was gone and New Year 1944 was here. January and February were quiet months but very cold. Snow covered the garden, making everything look white and peaceful. But it was far from peaceful in the city. The Germans were very nervous because the news from the Russian front was bad and the underground forces had sabotaged German installations and were killing high officers.

One day toward the end of February, just before 8 P.M., Anek rushed into the room, told me to put a coat on, not to take a thing with me, and not to ask any questions. We ran to Elki's place, which was about five blocks away. On the way Anek told me that one of the men from his group, who was a messenger and knew Kazia and Anek's addresses, had been arrested that afternoon. Nobody knew whether he had told the Germans what he knew. In any event both places were too dangerous to stay in. Once men were arrested they were tortured until they told the oppressors what they wanted to hear. If they did not come for Anek that night, it meant everything was all right.

We sat all night at Elki's apartment. At 6 A.M. Anek went back to the factory. He stayed at a distance and looked for unusual movement. The whole place might have been burned down. He came back and said that the place seemed quiet. It was dark and cold when we left Elki's. We stayed in the hallway of a house across the street from the factory and watched for anything unusual in or around the house. We could see the light in Mr. and Mrs. Wojciech's apartment. We could see the old lady walking around the room, probably preparing breakfast. We strained our eyes to see the garden, to see whether anything was there, maybe a shiny German helmet. Even though it seemed quiet, we could not be sure they were not waiting somewhere behind the bushes. We did not know whether they had interrogated the man during the night, though they usually did. It was really a stupid thing even to go close to the place. But we decided that if they had not come by now we would be safe.

We went home at about 7 A.M. Nobody had been there during the night, and nobody had asked for Anek.

The next day we found out that AK, through the men that worked in the prison, had given the prisoner breakfast with some poison in it. He died immediately without pain and had no chance to betray his squadron. Anek was notified right away that he and Kazia were safe.

I was not so sure. The next few nights I could not sleep, imagining noises. I thought I heard somebody walking on the roof or steps outside the windows.

chapter 15

$\mathcal{E}$aster came. Kazia brought us Easter baskets full of blessed multicolored eggs. We ate them and wished each other one thing: to survive this war. Anek brought me the most beautiful gift, a big bouquet of white lilacs, the first blooms from the garden. We had hardly even realized that spring was here again. Winter had passed and with it the cold winds and snow. The garden was growing greener every day and by Easter the lilacs were in full bloom.

Mr. and Mrs. Wojciech started to work in the garden all day long to prepare the earth for planting. I helped them around the house and sometimes cooked dinner for everybody. It was not difficult; it was soup every day. A year had passed since Anek had asked me to marry him in this garden, and a year had passed since I had lost my father. Sometimes it seemed as though it was only yesterday that I had left him and Grzybowska Street behind; the next day I would not be able to remember many things that had happened there. Anek was very good to me. He stayed with me all the time when he was not working and even then I could see him or hear him downstairs. Every evening, now that the weather was warm, we walked around the garden, and sometimes we ventured out to Elki's. She was a crazy, happy-go-lucky woman. She had lived in Kalisz, become a German citizen, and then became frightened and ran away to Warsaw, where she changed her name. Kazia had found her a job. She loved Kazia and would do anything for her. She knew who I was, but with her I was safe.

With the spring came the air raids. Russian planes bombarded Warsaw every night. We could not sleep at all, but everybody was happy that something was going on. We knew the Germans were losing on the eastern front and we knew that the Russians were slowly moving toward Warsaw.

A new law was passed. Every house was required to have a shelter equipped with food and water. Large apartment houses cleaned part of their basements and put in all the necessary supplies. Others dug large tunnels in gardens. They were more costly but safer. If a bomb hit an apartment house, all the rubble just cut off the flow of air to the basement shelters and people suffocated. In the factory, the workers started to dig a good-sized tunnel, reinforcing it with wooden columns and building wooden benches along its walls. It could hold about fifteen persons.

The air raids were becoming more frequent and lasted longer. At first we went to the shelter every time, but within a month we did not pay much attention to the sirens warning us that the planes were on the way. As soon as the sirens stopped, we could hear the planes. First they dropped flares or rockets. The whole city was lit up as if it were daytime so that they could see what to destroy. They tried to hit just the military targets, but it was impossible. Many houses were destroyed and many people died. The flares were extraordinary; they looked like an enormous bunch of grapes, and grew brighter closer to earth. Then at a certain moment the bombs started to fall. Meanwhile the German antiaircraft artillery would fire nonstop. The Russians threw fire from the sky, and the Germans fired toward the sky. The Russian planes flew too high for the artillery to reach them, and at night the gunners could not see where to aim.

Occasionally we also had daytime air raids. These were carried out by English planes, supposedly with Polish pilots from General Sikorski's army. They flew so high that we could hardly see them; they looked like small silver birds up in the sky. They were not bombing Warsaw, people said, they were dropping guns, ammunition, and food for the underground army that was being organized in the forests south of the city.

Evenings were growing warmer, and we spent more time in the garden helping Kazia dig and plant. The lilacs this year were full of blossoms and the daffodils were beautiful. Our room was full of them. They were my company during the day.

Anek worked very hard in those days. The factory had large orders to fill. Besides his work in the factory, he went to more and more secret meetings. Every time he ran in to change clothes and kiss me good-bye, my heart beat faster, worrying about what might happen to him, fearing that it might be the last time he kissed me. He was good to me, and continually told me that even though he could not take me with him to meetings or just to go out, he thought about me all the time he was away. Every time he came home he brought me some small thing that told me he had been thinking about me—chocolate, candy, or perhaps a piece of clothing.

The Russians were moving forward on the whole front. Some of the Germans felt that their end was near and tried to befriend their Polish enemies.

Wanda was as nice as she possibly could be to everybody. She felt, as they all did, that the ground was burning under her feet. She began telling stories against the Gestapo and the SS. One of them was her lover. At the end of June he was sent to the front and she left Warsaw to be with his family somewhere near Munich. A few days later the order came for all Germans not in uniform to evacuate the city. The Russians were advancing without meeting any resistance. The Germans began to move their offices. Senior officers packed their stolen belongings, including art objects, in order to send everything to the Fatherland. The air raids seemed never to stop. At night it was the Russians; in the daytime, the Allied forces. We were happy to hear them, to see them; it meant that the end of the war had to be near.

In the first week of July, Rita and her two children came to live with us. The Germans had built elaborate fortifications in her section of town, and she was afraid to stay there and possibly be cut off from the rest of the family. Kazia spent more and more time with us and soon moved in as well. Everybody was talking about an uprising. It was to take place the moment the Russians reached Praga, but nobody knew when that would happen.

Anek was so occupied with the AK that we hardly ever saw him at home. Sometimes he stayed away overnight, but I was not alone any more. The second floor of the factory was full of people. Rita and I liked each other the moment we met. Her children were so pretty—Lala was just two years old and Marek was five. Rita's hard life was visible in her face. Since the beginning of the war she had taken care of the family without her husband. I heard that even before the war he had not been a good provider and drank a lot.

chapter 16

*T*he first of August, 1944, started like any other pretty day. It was warm and sunny but we could feel a little nippy wind signaling an early Polish autumn. During the preceding few days everybody had been tense. Everyone knew something was about to happen, and we were all waiting for the Russians to cross the river and take Warsaw. Supposedly they were already in Praga (though in fact we learned later that they were still outside the city), but nobody knew why they were waiting there. German soldiers were nowhere to be seen. We did not know whether they were inside their barracks or had left the city. People who lived in the eastern part of Warsaw could hear tanks and trucks leaving the city day and night. The Germans had become so busy with the war that they left the Poles alone.

We lived, like everybody else, tense and waiting. We

knew the underground forces were ready and waiting, we just did not know the day or the hour. Every day we thought, but were afraid to say it out loud, that it would be "TODAY."

The "TODAY" came the first of August.

Anek came for lunch at twelve, as usual. We could see that he was very nervous; he did not eat at all. When we got up from the table, he embraced me, kissed me, and told us that he had received an order to report immediately to his post. He and Jan were to go to Koszykowa Street to join the others. He told Kazia never to leave me alone, and to take care of me until he came back.

"Take care of Lilly, Rita, and the kids. And do not leave this place. It will not last long. You have plenty to eat here, the garden is full of potatoes and vegetables. You can take everything you need from the factory. Wanda's reign is over."

He kissed his sisters and the children. Then he took my hand and we walked to the steps. I was so frightened and nervous that I could not say a word. He started to tell me, "If it is possible, I will come home tonight, but I think they will keep us at our post. Don't worry, darling. God willing, the whole thing will not last any longer than two or three days. When I come back I will never leave you alone. We will be free in free Poland. A few more days and all our troubles will be over, we will be together, together for our whole life."

One more kiss and he was gone. We all stayed at the window and watched him walking fast to the gate. He stopped, turned toward us, waved to us, sent us a kiss, and disappeared around the corner.

We sat on the bed looking at each other, unable to speak as we faced the knowledge that Anek had gone to fight the war, that anything could happen.

Just then Marysia came in, and when she looked at us, she knew something was happening. Rita explained. They decided that it would be wise to go to town and try to buy some more food. By the time they left, all the stores were closed, and people had started selling staples on the streets for extraordinary prices. They came home empty-handed.

Suddenly at 4 P.M. we heard people running on the street. We rushed to the window and saw men coming from every direction, running toward the center of town. Each had a rifle under his arm, and some were partially wrapped in paper or rugs. Gunfire began on all sides.

We could hear continuous machine-gun fire, explosions, and single shots. They came from far away; everything was going on downtown. Our neighborhood was quiet, we saw neither Germans nor our soldiers. From what little we heard, our organization had every advantage—good arms, wonderful soldiers fighting for their freedom, and not much opposition. Supposedly many German battalions had already left the city. Everyone was sure that in a day or two the Russians would cross the river and help to make Warsaw a free city. But we civilians and all the men in arms had been misled. How terribly misled the immediate future would show us.

That night when Rita fed the children and put them to bed, they cried a little—we were all very nervous and they could feel it. We all kissed them good night: Aunt Kazia, Aunt Marysia, and Aunt Stefcia (that was my name since I had obtained my *Kennkarte*—Stefania—Stefcia for short).

In the whole place only women were left except for old Mr. Wojciech. We all sat on the bed and listened for noises outside, hoping to hear Anek returning.

One day passed, then another. We had no news at all. From time to time we could see a man running on the street, probably a liaison man for our army. We heard continuous gunfire, but did not know who was winning.

Rita kept our spirits up. She was a very cheerful person, despite all she had been through. After the Germans took her husband to work on the German farms, she had lived on whatever Kazia and her brothers could give her. And that was barely enough for bread and beans.

The fourth and fifth day passed and we still had no news. We had plenty to eat. We started to dig out the potatoes, and vegetables and fruit were abundant. Once or twice we were able to stop a liaison man, but all he could tell us was that the posts were holding and the only thing that worried them was that the Russians had not crossed the river yet.

The good news did not last. After a week passed the firing became sporadic and we heard that the Germans were bringing back some forces in order to clean out the city. Under cover of tanks German soldiers took house after house, ran the civilians out, and set them afire. The news that reached us grew worse daily. The Germans brought in more and more soldiers and the Russians did not come. I could not understand what was going on; all I knew was that Anek had not come back.

Now Warsaw was one more casualty of this terrible war.

We listened to the sound of the machine guns as though they would tell us what was going on in the city. We saw more and more people running away with only small bundles of what they had been able to save. It was reported that our men were fighting without food or water. The expected help had never come. The sidewalks were said to be full of temporary graves and different groups were cut off from each other. Each man was fighting on his own and people were trying to leave the city through the sewers.

Day after day more refugees stopped at the factory. We gave them food and water. Some stayed overnight and all of them told us terrible news. They were all going somewhere to the countryside, as far away from the city as they could. Some of them had been helping our men to build barricades on the streets to stop the German tanks. They were not very effective; the men did not have enough material to build them with.

Meantime the sections of the city that were under German rule were "cleaned." The Germans announced that Warsaw would no longer exist and started to burn house after house and street after street. At night we could see bright flames reaching the sky all over the city. They were very thorough; they drove the people out, poured gasoline around the houses, and lighted them.

When the Germans came, they were sure no one would

shoot at them and that they could do their job in peace. What happened to the people depended on the officer in charge. They did not bother women much, but young men were a different story. Sometimes they shot them; sometimes they treated them as war prisoners, and sent them to war camps; sometimes they let them go with the women and children as long as they went as far as possible from the burning city.

Our section of town had not yet seen the action, but we stayed ready. Each of us had one bundle with clothes and one with food. Mrs. Wojciech baked bread every day, and we made some jelly from the green apples. We had enough food for ourselves and the people that stopped by. And there were more and more of them.

All our clothes—Anek's, Marysia's, mine, and Mr. and Mrs. Wojciech's—we put into a big box with steel sides and buried it in the garden, hoping that when it was all over we would have something to wear.

As the ring of fire closed around us, two families from the next house came over to ask if they could stay in the factory. They considered our place safer. They spoke to Rita about taking the children in their arms when the Germans came, and that was arranged. Both men were in their late thirties, and like all of us, frightened. One of the men, Jurek, was very nervous. He could not sit still, and paced back and forth across the room continually. He did not want to stay in his apartment. When he was in the factory, he spent most of his time in the bomb shelter. During the first days of the uprising we had all spent a great deal of time in the "hole," but as the days passed we stayed there less and less. When we were upstairs we were careful not to approach the windows because there were stray bullets flying around.

It was the tenth of August. We could hear shots, but they were sparse. Jurek wanted to walk in the garden for a while, to breathe some fresh air. His wife talked him out of it. He was walking toward the window when suddenly we heard a shot, a dry "paf." Jurek threw his hands to his chest and screamed, "They shot me! Help me! Save me!"

We did not know whether the shot was a stray or had been aimed at him. It had gone through Jurek, made a hole in the door, and lodged in the wall. Jurek, a tall, muscular man, fell like weed cut down with a scythe.

We all panicked. Nobody knew how to help him and we did not know where to look for a doctor. Kazia was the only one who had taken a Red Cross course. She tore off his shirt and cleaned the wound, but she could not stop the flow of blood. Marysia and I ran outside, she to the right and I to the left, looking for a doctor, but we could not find one. When we came back, Jurek was lying in the same place, very quiet, blood oozing from his wound. Kazia was changing the dressings, but it did not help; it seemed to me that the narrow streak of blood was growing wider. After a short while Jurek complained that his hands and feet were cold, then he lost consciousness. We put hot compresses to his feet and hands but it did not help; he was bleeding internally. Blood started to pour from his nose and mouth. A few minutes later he was dead.

That same night, with the help of his wife, we dug a deep, narrow grave, wrapped the body in a sheet, and buried him. We all cried, but tried to be quiet so as not to awaken the children. Our grief, though, could not compare with what the wife felt. I don't think she realized what she was doing while she was digging the hole that was for her husband. She made a wooden cross, carved his full name on it, and pushed it into the soft earth. Her hands were shaking so much that the letters came out very uneven, but she wanted to do it.

We did not have much time to think about it all. The ring of fire was approaching. The Germans had started to "clean" Niepodleglosci Street; we were next. Smoke was rolling into the room, and only when the wind blew the other way could we breathe easier. We were ready. The day before they had set fire to the houses one block away; we knew we were next. The smoke was so thick that we could hardly see the trees in the garden. We closed all the windows and that helped a little. The air was much cleaner in the front of the building, but we were afraid to go out there.

The next morning we put our bundles next to the door in order to be able to get out as fast as possible. We did not wait long. At about seven o'clock the trucks full of Germans began to arrive. They ran in the houses with machine guns ready to shoot. We could hear shouts of *"raus,"* *"raus,"* from everywhere. Men were ordered to keep their arms high in the air. The Germans were acting just as they had in the ghetto; the only difference was that they did not take people to the *Umschlagplatz.* We ran out as fast as possible, taking with us everything we could, as we knew we would not see this place again.

We had only two men in the house. One was old Mr. Wojciech and the other took Lala in his arms as he was leaving. Lala, seeing these strange people running about, screamed the whole time. We could not find Mr. Wojciech, and then we remembered; we had talked about opening the rabbit cages so that they could get out. Otherwise they would starve. He had gone to do it. If the Germans spotted him there, they would surely kill him. We were all standing in the street, waiting for the people from the other houses, when we saw him sneaking from the back to join us. One soldier noticed him and started to shout at him, but smart grandpa touched his ear as though he were deaf, and the German just pushed him toward the group.

When they had decided it was time, the Germans escorted us out of town. "Just go—go forward and don't look back." When we reached the outskirts of town, the Germans returned to help their comrades set fire to the newly empty houses.

We were out of town. Behind us was burning Warsaw, in front of us open fields. People dispersed in all directions. Whoever had a family or friends in the country tried to get to them.

chapter 17

*W*e walked for a while, Kazia, Rita with the children, Marysia, and I. The day was clear and warm and as noon approached the sun heated up. The bundles on our backs grew heavier. Near the Okecie Airfield, people had planted small plots of land with all sorts of fruits and vegetables. We sat under a tree, ate some fruit, and had to decide which way to go. We would have liked to take some food with us but we could not carry any more. From far away we could see the smoke floating over the city. Somewhere there Anek was fighting for a cause without hope of winning. And now we were leaving. If he came back, how would he know where we were? We knew that a few posts were still fighting, but they were surrounded and could not hold out much longer.

Kazia decided we should go to Pyry. A few months

earlier Elki had moved there. She had not liked living in the big city. After the incident with Anek, when we ran to her apartment and stayed there overnight, she became more frightened and moved to the country. Pyry had once been a summer resort. We did not know exactly how far we would have to walk, but having a goal gave us more strength.

We did not have Elki's address; we were not even sure if she still lived there, but we had to try. We took back roads. There were people everywhere and German cars passing by, trailing clouds of dust. The little villages on the way were full of refugees and soldiers. Germans had battalions stationed all around Warsaw and requisitioned food from the farmers. The poor people had only what they could hide. What could they share with all these tired and hungry refugees?

At noon we could walk no longer. The children were crying; they were thirsty and hungry. We sat in the shade of a big tree because the sun had been beating down on us unmercifully. While Rita and Marysia stayed with the children and watched over our belongings, Kazia and I went around knocking on doors, asking for water and maybe some milk for the children. Every farmer had a house full of people and very little food. Finally we did get some water and some fruit. After we had rested for a while, we were up and walking again.

We reached Pyry in the early evening. It was a very small town with one main street, but quite a few houses scattered around. From the first house on the main street we started to ask for Elki. Somebody must know her and where she lived. She was not a quiet or shy person. She was a good-looking blonde with a big mouth; somebody had to know her.

We found her. She and her daughter Irene lived in a nice, clean brick house. She had a two-room apartment on the first floor. The rest of the house was occupied by officers of the Gestapo. They had left her there because she was useful to them—she spoke German and cleaned and washed for them. She was delighted to see us. She said she had sent Irene to the main street every day to look for somebody from the family. She had been hoping we would come that way.

We sat down on the front steps, hardly able to move. Elki deluged us with questions, but we did not have many answers. After we had rested for a while, we went one by one to wash up. Rita fed the children and put them to bed. We all sat around the table, ate dinner—oh, this soup really tasted good—and debated what to do next. There was not much we could do; we would stay with Elki for the time being. Having a place to stay was a blessing.

We went to sleep very early that night. Elki and her daughter slept in one bed, Kazia in the other bed, and Marysia opened a cot for herself. In the kitchen, a fairly large room, Rita and her children slept in one wide bed and I took a narrow one. It was very, very comfortable. We were too tired to hear the German boots thumping to and fro on the upper floor.

The next day Kazia and Marysia went to look for food. Elki went to work upstairs, and Rita and I stayed home with Lala and Mark. It was better for me to stay inside as much as possible. There were Gestapo agents everywhere and I did not want to take chances. But I was more free in Pyry than ever before; I was part of a big family and I felt safe. In these circumstances people were not interested in what the neighbors were doing, they were too busy just staying alive.

Lala and Mark called me Aunt Stefa. I played with them every free moment and, of course, they loved it. Rita and I shared the chores of house cleaning, washing, and cooking.

Every day Kazia and Marysia went to the farmers around Pyry looking for anything that could be eaten. Sometimes they were lucky and the farmers let them dig some potatoes or buy some bacon. Most of the potatoes and vegetables had not been harvested and were just rotting in the ground. The German soldiers went around every day and took everything they could find. Some farmers let the refugees dig out whatever they wanted and refused money, but asked help in plowing the fields or caring for the animals.

Every day we had soup for lunch and dinner. Every day I peeled the potatoes and Rita cooked. Sometimes we had a few beans in the soup, sometimes some turnips, and sometimes some bread and bacon grease. Kazia had to stand in line and wait for hours to get a loaf of bread, but it was worth it.

One good thing was that we were warm. Elki had a lot of coal put away, and we all gathered wood in a nearby forest. We kept a fire in the stove throughout the day and the soup was always hot.

The officers upstairs knew that Elki had her family from Warsaw with her. We were terrified of them, but they were almost polite to us. After a few days they told Elki we could stay but that we would have to work for them. From time to time they brought things to be washed or asked for hot coffee.

The news we could gather from Warsaw was the worst. The Germans had given the remaining fighters an ultimatum and told them they would treat them as prisoners of war. After two weeks of fighting with no hope of help, they surrendered! The survivors were taken to the German camps, and the rest of downtown Warsaw was "cleaned" with fire. The Russians were still across the river, looking at the burning city, as they said later, preparing for the spring offensive.

The day before the surrender we heard English planes flying over. We could tell who the planes belonged to by the sound of their engines. They looked like tiny silver birds. When they flew away, we could still see small dark dots in the sky. Little by little the dots grew larger and larger until we could see that they were different colors. The men knew what they were. It was help for the soldiers of the uprising— but it was too late. The sky was full of bright-colored parachutes. Red for ammunition, white for food, we thought, but nobody knew for sure because most of them were picked up by the Germans. They hit one plane; we could see it going down in smoke. Some people said that they had seen the pilot bailing out. Everybody left their doors open during the night, in case he looked for shelter. But we never knew what

Winter 1937: A friend, Aunt Lunia, and I skating in Kalisz on the Prosna River.

Summer 1937: The whole family on summer vacation. *Front row, left to right:* Aunt Lula, me, Aunt Bertha (Lunia's twin sister), Cousin Irene, and a neighbor; *center:* Uncle Josef (Mother's brother), Grandmother Helena, Grandfather Max, my mother; *back row:* Grandmother Maria, Uncle Wladek, Lunia, and my father.

Fall 1937: On the balcony of Grandmother Maria's apartment. Grandmother Maria, Grandfather Max and his wife, Helena, and me.

Fall 1937: Marysia and her dog on the balcony of Grandmother Maria's apartment.

Fall 1938: Me with my new bicycle.

Spring 1939: My father, a friend, Aunt Bertha, and my mother strolling in Krynica, one of the best-known health spas in Poland.

Warsaw, 1939: Rita and her son.

Warsaw, sometime before 1939:
Kazia and Mr. Dymski.

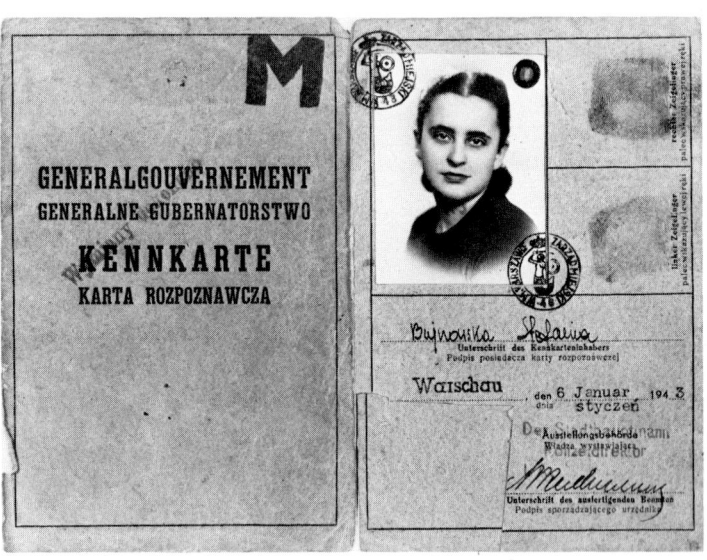

Warsaw, 1943: My counterfeit identity card.

Warsaw, 1944: Anek and I on one of the very few walks I took during that year.

Kalisz, spring 1945: On vacation in Jelenia Gora.

Berlin, 1946: Me in uniform, riding a motorcycle with another of Chaplain Shubow's workers.

Berlin, spring 1946: Me just before I left Germany.

Marine Fletcher, the ship that carried me from Europe.

Arriving in New York harbor, with the Statue of Liberty showing faintly behind me.

happened to him. He could have been killed by German fire or died when he hit the earth.

These episodes kept our hopes alive. There was somebody, somewhere, who cared a little. People said that the pilots were Poles from the army of General Sikorski. But our boys needed more than a few boxes of ammunition; they needed manpower and had not received it.

Day after day passed as we lived in hope of hearing some news from Anek or his brother. I did not go out much, but stayed home and took care of the children. They really loved me. All day long they wanted me to read to them or play with them. Rita had a happy nature. She kept our spirits up, singing all the time and telling us that things would soon be better.

Our Gestapo neighbors wanted more people to work for them. Besides Elki, Kazia, Marysia, and I were taking different shifts. They needed help around the clock; some of the officers were leaving, and new ones were arriving. They wanted clean linens, warm water, coffee. One day they told Elki that they would be giving a big party the following Saturday. It was to be in the villa of one of the captains and they wanted Miss Stefi (that was me) to help with choosing the menu and arranging the tables. They also said it would continue later than 8 P.M. but that they would provide an escort to take me home. I was afraid to go, but I had no choice. I was not worried about the Germans, but we did not know who else might be there.

Saturday noon we went to work. Elki was in charge of the kitchen, I was to set the tables and decorate the rooms. We took Elki's daughter with us. If we could steal some food, Irene would take it home. They had enormous amounts of food—ham, sausages, cheeses, butter, whole loins of beef and pork. In the kitchen Elki had two soldiers helping her, peeling potatoes, bringing wood—the hard work. The irony of it: I had two soldiers to help me—I was telling them what to do. They were just like any young boys, far from home, trying to be pleasant—to me.

The villa had belonged to a wealthy Polish industrialist who had left everything behind: beautiful china, crystal, pure linen tablecloths. The furniture was exquisite, the living room furnished with Louis XVI pieces.

The present owner of this beautiful villa was one of the highest Gestapo officers in the area. He came over and told me please to do my best; if I needed more help, he would send me more soldiers. "No, no more, everything will be fine!" I said.

I sent the soldiers to get some evergreens and flowers, whatever they could get—imagine me giving orders to German soldiers! I set up a bar on one side of the room, a long table on another side, and a few small tables in the middle. All were covered with white tablecloths and each had a flower arrangement. We had to wash all the china and crystal, but by six o'clock everything was ready. When we started to put all the cold cuts and salads on the dining room table, Mr. Big came, dressed in gala uniform, full of medals, smelling of strong cologne. He liked what we had done. Elki was still in the kitchen, cutting the meat and putting it on platters in the oven so that everything would be warm.

At about seven the officers started to gather. There were no civilians and no women. We were nearly ready to leave when Mr. Big asked us to start to pour champagne and whiskey. I was becoming frightened, but the Germans were polite. When they had all arrived and everyone had a glass in hand, Mr. Big gave me a glass and asked me to toast with them to Hitler's health and sing with them "*Deutschland, Deutschland Uber Alles.*"

I did not know what to do. I resisted a strong urge to throw the glass of champagne at them, and I drank but did not sing. I emptied the glass to the last drop wishing for a free Poland and death to all the Germans.

They must have known how I felt, how any Pole would feel. I suppose in that moment they did not think about war. They probably wanted to forget it. Dunces, they did not know with whom they were toasting Hitler's health. And I hoped they would never find out.

After they had finished singing their anthem, I went to Mr. Big and told him very nicely but very firmly that I had finished my job and wanted to be taken home. He looked at me a little surprised and said, "Look at all the good food we have here. I know you cannot buy it. We will bring some girls later and then the party will really start." I looked at him and smiled, so that he knew I understood what he meant. I very firmly thanked him for the offer to spend a gay night but I wanted to go home now. He called one of the soldiers and told him to take me home.

I was amazed at my own strength. Walking back home I thought about what could have happened if they had not let me go. I imagine he did not want to create a scene in front of the others, but the important thing for me was that he sent me home. Everyone was worried about me at home; they knew what went on at those kinds of parties. I think if I had waited until they had had a few drinks, they might not have let me leave so easily.

chapter 18

The next night something strange happened to me. It was not a dream: it was very real. We all went to bed early, as usual. My bed was close to the light switch, so I was the one who always turned it off. Rita and the children slept close by. We said our good night, I turned the light off, covered myself, and tried to go to sleep. A moment later I felt somebody standing close to my bed. It was dark and I could not see a thing, but I could feel a presence. I was frightened and began to perspire; then I felt somebody bending closer to me. I wanted to scream, but my voice did not come out. I wanted to reach for the light switch but I could not move. I felt human breath close to me. I lifted my hand from under the cover and tried to push it away and I touched something hard—it felt like teeth. In that moment I knew it was Anek,

I was sure it was he. But I could not see him. I pulled the covers over my head and waited. I was so frightened I did not know what to do. I don't know how long I stayed under the covers, but I finally fell asleep.

When I awakened the next morning, I asked Rita if she had heard anything during the night. Any unusual noise? She had not heard a thing or seen a thing. Meanwhile Kazia and Elki came to the kitchen and I told them what had happened to me the night before. Everyone had a different interpretation. Elki said, "I can only interpret it this way. Anek is dead. He came to Lilly to tell her good-bye."

We all thought the same way but did not want to say it. I knew it had not been a dream.

Everybody was very nervous that day. We were waiting for something to happen, some news to come. We were hoping to hear something from Anek or Jan.

We heard a rumor that somebody had received postcards from the soldiers of the uprising. We did not see any. In Pyry we had no radio, no newspapers. We only knew what somebody told somebody.

At the end of October Elki procured a pass for us to go to Warsaw and see if we could salvage something from our homes, mine and Kazia's. Three of us went—Kazia, Marysia, and I. We left Pyry early in the morning with some empty bags and a little baby carriage, to make it easier to bring back as much as we could. The city was empty. Nobody could enter without a special pass. The law required us to walk in the middle of the streets. Hundreds of people came to the city without a permit just to steal whatever they found of any value. Many of them found a lot: money, jewelry, not to mention all kinds of clothes. It was, of course, against the law to steal and whoever was caught was killed on the spot.

We reached the city about 9 A.M. It was an unusually warm autumn day, and we were tired and hot. It was much cooler in the shadows of the buildings. The streets were empty, the houses on both sides of the streets looked like skeletons, burned, black from smoke. From time to time we saw cadavers lying on the street and the smell was just terrible. I imagine they had been killed when caught looting, and nobody took care of the bodies. We had to hold our breath when we passed them; the stench was overpowering.

First we went to the factory. It had been completely destroyed. The Germans or the looters had dug up our boxes, and pieces of clothing were strewn everywhere. They must have noticed fresh dirt and thought something really valuable was buried there—the whole garden had been dug up. The only place they had not touched was the grave. The flowers that Jurek's wife had put on the grave were dry and brown, but they had not been bothered. The rabbits must have multiplied since Mr. Wojciech had given them their freedom. We could see numerous rabbit holes around the yard and little ones hopped among the bushes. There was nothing we could do or find in the factory. The next stop was Kazia's apartment. To get there we had to cross Aleja Niepodleglosci, a wide street with German barracks at one end, so that they could see what was going on on that street. We walked in the middle of the street, quickly but not running. Only when we reached Kazia's street did we breathe a little easier. Her house had not been burned but her apartment had been ransacked. The pillows had been torn open and feathers were everywhere. We found very few things worth taking back to Pyry. Winter was coming and we wanted to bring some sweaters and warm coats for the children, for Rita, and for us. We decided to look in other houses that had not been burned. It was looting, but if we did not take those things, the Germans would, we reasoned. We talked about it for a while. It was a very hard decision to make and a dangerous one. We decided to stop in one of the houses on the way back toward Pyry. It was a large house and the Germans had not "cleaned" it yet. We could see through the windows that there were clothes everywhere.

Our hearts pounded as we walked in. The doors to all the apartments were open. We could not believe our eyes. There were beautiful clothes all over the floor, beds, chairs.

In one room all we could see were furs—silver fox capes, full-length seal coats. We just looked at each other. We did not want furs, we did not want to get those things and sell them, we just wanted some warm things for the family. We went to another apartment and we found some warm underwear and some overcoats. We wore what we could and we put the rest in our bags. We had forgotten the little carriage we took with us from Pyry in Kazia's apartment.

On the way back we did not speak at all. I felt the whole of Poland must know what I had done. I had taken an old coat for myself. The rest was for the children, Rita, Elki, and her daughter. We reached home without any trouble. Everybody in Pyry had been very nervous waiting for us. Even though we had all the papers, nothing was safe. Rita cried when she saw us coming. Everybody was happy with what we had brought.

A few more days passed and we still had no news from the world and, more importantly, from Anek. We could think about nothing else and waited uneasily for what the next day would bring.

In the middle of November the German high command moved to Pyry. They took all the rooms that were decent and ours belonged in that category. We had to leave. Thanks to Elki and people she knew we found a little room in the attic of a two-story bungalow. All the other rooms had been taken by the army. The owners had permission to live in two little rooms in the attic, and they let us have one of them. We had three cots to sleep on. Kazia slept with Lala, Rita with her son Mark, and I got Marysia. We had a very small iron stove that could heat one pot.

The days were growing colder and our big problem was how to keep warm. It was impossible to buy coal. We all went to the edge of the forest to gather pine cones and twigs, but they burned very fast and did not give much warmth. Sometimes the farmers gave us wood in exchange for some clothes, but it was so wet that we got more smoke than fire. Kazia and Marysia went to the highway to wait there for passing coal wagons and picked up every little piece that fell off. If they were lucky they came home with a bagful; sometimes they only brought a few small pieces. They were not the only ones there, the roads were full of children and adults waiting for the same thing.

Since we had arrived in Pyry, Marysia and I had lived in peaceful coexistence. Kazia was the boss and we all knew it. We all had the same worry—how to survive. We were all busy with different chores. Kazia and Marysia were hardly ever home during the day; they stayed in lines for bread or coffee, which were both rationed. The bread was worse every day; it was not baked long enough and remained sticky inside. I could hardly swallow it, and the coffee with saccharin left a sour aftertaste. We did not know which was worse. When Rita and I stayed home alone we sometimes "snitched" a piece of bacon (it was saved for soup) and made a sandwich. We felt very badly about it after the fact; we felt like we had let the family down. When the room was cold we often went to bed and just talked for hours. Rita and I became very good friends. She was like a sister to me. Living in such a small room it was easy to get on each other's nerves, but we never quarreled. We comforted each other. She was waiting for some news from her husband and I was waiting for a word from Anek. Her husband, Stasiek, had been taken to Germany to work in the fields at the beginning of 1942. He wrote to her. The last letter had come just before the uprising. He had Elki's address and Rita was hoping he would try to find out from Elki where everybody was. We imagined he did not have the true picture of what was happening in Warsaw.

Rita told me about the wonderful letters he had written to her—how terrible he felt that he could not help her, that he was so far away; he wanted her to sell everything from the house for food to keep the children and her in good health. He said when all this mess was over he would work hard to buy all the things they needed.

At the end of November 1944 a letter came. Stasiek wrote to Elki hoping that she knew where his family was and asking her to deliver this letter to them or write him back telling him where they were. He wrote that Jan had gotten in touch with him. Jan was in the prisoner of war camp. He said that Anek had been killed defending the barricade on the fifth day of the uprising. Jan was with him when he died and had buried him in the little garden on Mokotowska Street. They had both been fighting on the barricade next to the Plaza of Three Crosses. Anek was hit in the stomach by machine-gun fire. Jan and their commander dragged him away to a nearby house, but could not save him. Before he went into a coma he had told them to take care of me. They had to promise him that when the war was over they would find me and take care of me as the wife of a soldier who died defending his country.

We read and reread the letter, crying until we had no tears left. I think Rita had had more hope that Anek was alive than I. I had felt he would not come back to me. One day I was sure of it, then the next I had hope, just a little hope that he would come back, that we would both survive and have a life together when the war was over. Elki was right. That night when I felt Anek came to me, he had come to say good-bye.

Now I could not live with any hope. I had lost the man who was everything to me. He had helped me to survive the most difficult days of my life. Who would help me now to survive this tragedy? Kazia and Rita sat next to me and we all cried together. They told me again and again that they would not leave me, that they would take care of me and share the last piece of bread with me until this hell was over.

And they fulfilled this promise. Kazia was our guardian angel, she was the head of the family. Rita was like a sister. I never felt that I was an outsider. In fact, I was somebody they risked their lives for every day. They shared with me one slice of bread or one bowl of soup and I never forgot it.

We went to bed early that day. It was very cold and when you slept you could not feel how hungry you were. But I could not sleep. I wanted to cry a little longer but did not want to keep the others awake. Tears were running, the pillow was getting wet, and I could not stop. All sorts of thoughts crossed my mind. I loved them all but I was just one more mouth to feed; maybe it would be better if I volunteered for farm labor in Germany. It would be safer for all of them.

The next day I told them what I had decided to do. Everybody started to talk at once. "You must be crazy," Kazia said. "We went through so much together, and now that winter is almost over, spring will bring the Russians. We will be free, we will have more food. Anek would never forgive us if we let you go. Just forget it, it was a rotten idea. The case is closed."

The winter was not over and spring was still far away. The roads and fields were covered with a thick layer of snow. Freezing wind painted our cheeks red. The room was almost as cold as outside, so Rita, the children, and I went into the fields and built snowmen. But when you play outside, you get hungry. That was the worst part of playing outside. Food was more and more difficult to find.

chapter 19

One beautiful, sunny, but very cold morning in January 1945 (we really had not noticed how beautiful it was because we were freezing in bed) we heard movement on the highway. It meant one thing: the Germans were withdrawing from Pyry and the surrounding areas. We ran out to look and ask questions. They were taking horses and wagons from the farmers, piling on them what they could, and running west. Heavy artillery, tanks, cars of all sizes and descriptions, everything was going west. That was it, the Russians were moving forward. The Germans passed through Pyry all day and all night, just a long line of people and machinery. The next day the high command left. One of the officers came to Elki to say good-bye. He was polite, and told her they would be back soon. But as Elki told us later, he did not look like he meant it. We had to wait for hours, almost until night fell, before we could cross the highway to go back to our place with Elki. Her apartment was a haven, warm and clean. The Germans had left a large supply of coal, the stove was hot, the coffee tasted delicious. We sat around the table the whole night, waiting. The traffic on the highway stopped and we heard shots, but from far away. Now that the Germans were gone, the Russians would come without a fight. We heard that the division that had left Pyry was destroyed near Lowicz.

The next morning, around ten o'clock, we heard the sound of heavy wheels on the road, and after a few minutes the first Russian tanks entered Pyry. Everyone stayed home and watched from behind their curtains to see what would happen next. If fighting started, we were ready to run to the basement.

The tanks were enormous, looking more than two stories high. Suddenly they stopped, a few soldiers came out, talked to each other, and stamped their feet to warm up. A short while later, we heard a voice speaking very clearly in Polish. It was an order from the commander to the civilian population. We were not to go out on the streets for a few more hours, because they were unsure whether some Germans were not hiding in the nearby forest. Otherwise everybody was free and could go to their homes as soon as possible. Then he said that after the tanks moved ahead the Polish army was coming.

From afar we could hear the noise of the planes. In a few minutes we could see them coming out of the clouds. The soldiers stood by the tanks looking up because they were their planes. But suddenly the planes came down and started to shoot at them. Every one of the soldiers dived under the tanks, the planes flew away, then came back again once more and were gone. After a while the loudspeaker came on again and told us that the Russian planes had made a mistake, that it happened often when the front moved so fast.

In the early afternoon the tanks moved west and the infantry moved in. That is how the first day under Russian occupation passed. It was the first day I was free; I could go out and tell everybody who I was. No Gestapo or concentration camp hung over my head.

We waited a week before we decided to go to Warsaw and see if it was possible to live there. We knew Kazia's apartment had been saved but we had to find out what had happened to Rita's place. Kazia and I decided to go to Praga and see.

We could not use the highways; the soldiers said some were still full of mines. We decided to go through the fields. Polish winters are cold, windy, and snowy, this one was a little worse than some, or maybe we felt the cold more. We were undernourished and not properly dressed, even though we had put on layers and layers of clothes. The snow was deep and it was a slow walk. We were a little afraid to walk alone, so after a while we joined a group of men and women who were going in the same direction. Finally we came to the river Wisla. Praga was on the other side, but the two big bridges were gone. The Germans had blown them up before leaving. Only twisted metal and piles of rubble were left. They had even mined the ice on the river, but since then the river had frozen again and all of us decided to cross it. It would have been pretty easy if the ice had been flat, but the explosions had formed little mountains in the middle of the river and we had to walk zig-zagging. We walked interminably before we finally arrived in the section of Praga where Rita's in-laws lived.

Praga had not suffered at all. The stores were open, and the streets were full of people. Men were cleaning the snow off the sidewalks. It seemed like the war had been over for years in this part of town.

First we went to Rita's in-laws' place. Her mother-in-law was at home. They had not lost a thing, they had never left the apartment, and did not know and could not imagine what our lives had been during all this time. The mother-in-law told us that Rita's apartment was fine, nothing was stolen. They had kept an eye on it the whole time. She also said that many people had come to live in Praga from the other side of the river, and when they saw an empty place they just moved in. Food was becoming more expensive because the merchants took it to Warsaw where they could charge whatever they wanted. "It is a shame," she said, "that Rita and the children did not stay home, they would have been safer here." The lady was very nice to us. We stayed there for two days and rested and ate a lot to build up our strength for the trip back.

In the middle of February Rita and the children went to her home. Kazia took Marysia and me to her apartment, and Elki and her daughter stayed in Pyry. They had all kinds of food and plenty of coal left by the Germans. Before we actually moved to Warsaw, we went there every day to clean the apartment. Just being there was enough to warn people that the owners had come back. If the place was empty, anyone could move in and no law could make them move. The city was in ruins. People returning had no place to live. The city had no water and no electricity. Everyone who lived in the city was required to work a specified number of hours cleaning the rubble from the streets so that traffic could be restored more or less to normal.

To get water we had to go to the pump two blocks away and wait in line. Sometimes I came home without the water because the pump had run dry. We melted snow and ice for washing and for the toilet.

The streets were full of people, but it was difficult to imagine where they lived. If it was barely possible to make a room habitable, people did it. Very few were as lucky as we were. All we had to do was board up the broken windows. We had beds, chairs, tables, dishes, a stove—all the necessities of life.

Most returning residents were forced to work for days before their repairs made their places livable. They searched the ruins for building materials, using old bricks and half-burned wood. We often saw a completely burned house with a newly built room somewhere in the rear where the family lived. The downtown was in ashes. Street after street was completely in rubble. It was very dangerous to walk close to the ruins because when the wind blew strongly, pieces of brick flew everywhere.

Shortly after we returned to the city, Kazia and I went to look for Anek's grave. We knew, more or less, where he had been killed. We began looking around the Plaza of Three Crosses and Mokotowska Street. The sidewalks and little gardens were full of graves. Some had crosses with names on them, some had nothing. The places where the fight had been bloodiest had the most graves. It did not take us long to find the grave we were looking for. It was in a small garden on Mokotowska Street and it had a cross with his name carved on it. We had no doubt that it was Anek buried there. We stood there in that quiet little garden for a long time. We did not talk; we just wept. People passed by, like us, looking for graves of their loved ones. They thought we were lucky to find "our grave." Many of them would never know where their loved ones had been put to rest. Those who had died in the first days of the uprising were buried in individual graves, but later, when there were more casualties and less time, they were buried in mass graves and often with no names.

The government informed the public that in the spring, families could dig up the bodies and take them to the military cemetery for burial. Graves without names would be taken care of by the government. Those bodies would be taken to a specially built mausoleum.

In the beginning of March Marysia and I decided to go to Kalisz to see what was left of my family's properties. Passenger trains were not running yet, but the military transport trains took civilians who wanted to go to their hometowns. There were hundreds of people waiting for this kind of transportation.

I said good-bye to Kazia, promising her that I would be back when it was time to move Anek's body to his final resting place. Words could not express what I felt. How could

I just say thank you to her. How can you ever repay some-body who saved your life, at the same time endangering her own. We were both crying, but we were happy that we both had made it, and we were to be back together in a month or two.

We were lucky enough to get on a freight train. Before the war it had been a cattle train, during the war it had been used to transport soldiers, and now it was used for whatever was necessary. We climbed into a dark car that looked almost empty. Then we noticed a small iron stove with a few soldiers and civilians sitting around it. They looked at two helpless women and let us in. Marysia was terrified. We had heard about rapes taking place on the trains. It was cold in the car, and the men sat close to the fire without paying much atten-tion to us. We did not look very interesting, with our bulky coats and heavy woolen shawls wrapped around us—anything but sexy. The trip should have taken about six to eight hours; it took two days and two nights. The train would stop for hours in the middle of nowhere, waiting for more important transports to pass by. After the first day, the trip grew worse by the minute. There was not enough wood to keep the little stove burning all the time. At night we sat close together to keep warm, afraid to fall asleep, keeping watch over our meager belongings. Our companions left the train at different stops, until finally we had only three soldiers with us. The bread we had with us was gone, we had to move around to keep warm, and we thought this trip would never end. Finally, after two days, very early in the morning, we arrived in Kalisz.

We had about a twenty-minute walk from the station to the Rypinek section of town, where, we were hoping, Marysia's cousin Janka still lived. We were chilled to the bone and hungry when we arrived in Kazimierz and Janka's house. Janka almost fainted when she saw us. They fed us a big breakfast, we talked a little, and then we went to sleep. We slept for twenty-four hours in a clean warm bed.

The city had not been ruined. The Germans had left in

such a hurry that they had had no time to mine the roads or the buildings. However, they did take with them any movable objects from the houses they had occupied. In the time between their escape and the entrance of the Russians, thieves took the rest. Many of the naturalized Germans, the *Volksdeutsche*, stayed. They had no place to run to, and they were the ones people turned against. Most of them were put in jails, to be tried later.

Little by little, prewar residents began to return. The apartments evacuated by the Germans were occupied by the first arrivals, but after a few days the temporary government sealed empty apartments and houses. They were to be claimed by the rightful owners. If people could find their furniture, wherever it might be, they were entitled to a permit to move it to their dwelling.

My apartment had already been taken by someone, but our possessions were not there. I did not try to claim my apartment legally; it was too big for me anyway. I wanted the apartment where my grandmother Maria had lived. It had also been taken, but if I really needed it, I could legally get it. The people would have to move. The housing officials asked me if I would take the same size apartment one floor below. I agreed. It did not make much difference; both apartments had a few pieces of furniture, but none that had belonged to my grandmother.

It was a nice, clean place, full of sunshine. It was furnished with a bed, a little table, and a wardrobe in what became my bedroom, and an old sofa in the other room. The kitchen was in working order and the bathroom looked beautiful.

Shortly after we moved in, my old nurse came home. Michasia had lived through the war working as a maid for the Germans. She had no family and no place to stay. It was natural to ask her to stay with me. She looked very old and worn out and lost. She had taken care of me from the time I was born. It was my turn now to take care of her. The apartment had a little room next to the kitchen and that was where she slept. Marysia was not happy with this arrangement. She had never liked my nurse. It was a mutual feeling; there was always a rivalry between those two. Now Marysia was worried that I would give Michasia money. She wanted it all for herself, but in those days I did not have much. My poor nurse was not very smart, but she had a heart of gold. The Germans she had worked for had taken everything with them, even her clothes, and she was frightened to do anything about it.

We stayed up late for the first few nights talking. For the most part I talked, telling her what had happened to our family from the time we had said good-bye in August of 1939 until now. She cried the whole time and I joined her.

I was happy with my apartment. I was on my own, but the little money we had was fast disappearing. Marysia said that she had nothing more to sell. I had to start making something—we had to eat.

Michasia went to work cleaning apartments for new tenants but made barely enough to feed herself. After a few days she realized the work was just too hard for her. She was too old and worn out and her mind was failing a little. She was very forgetful and talked about the same thing over and over. She liked to talk about the time when I was a baby, and all the clever things I did when I started school, the day I received my first bicycle—I thought then it was the happiest day of my life. One thing she had saved from the Germans was a picture album of me, from the time I was born until I started school. Now she gave it to me. These were the only pictures of me and my family, the only things I had that I could look at and feel I was close to them. When Michasia and I sat together and talked, Marysia always seemed to be close by. She did not want us to be alone. The only reason I could think of was that she did not want me to tell Michasia about her. It was very irritating and I did not know what to do about it.

It was Michasia's home also and I could not just tell her

to leave. The tension was terrible. I knew Marysia wanted me to tell my nurse to move out or look for another job, but I would not do it. A few days later, Michasia decided to visit some distant cousins who lived in a little village not far from Kalisz. She said she would go there for a few weeks to rest and then she would come back when I was more settled and had a job. In a way I was happy she had made the decision by herself. She was perceptive enough to feel the tension, she knew I did not have my own money, and she did not want Marysia to feed her. I wanted her to come back and she knew it. I knew that she would be back. Her nature was to protect me, and she knew I would need protection from Marysia sooner or later.

Day after day we searched for the furniture from my family's apartment, or those of my grandparents, with no luck. Marysia remembered that we had left the sewing machine with a family that became *Volksdeutsche*. I went to their apartment and told them that I wanted the machine back. The man was afraid of his own shadow and gave it to me without an argument. He did not even ask if I had a permit from the agency to take it.

Before we had left Kalisz, mother had taken some curtains, linens, pillows, and blankets to the farmer we used to spend summers with. I rented a wagon and we went there, fourteen kilometers on terrible back roads. The farmer and his family had been certain nobody would return. When they saw us, they thought they were hallucinating. First they said the Germans had taken everything, and then that they had had to sell our things for food. After a long conversation they gave me back part of the things we had left. I was happy with what I received.

Some people we met gave us a table and a few chairs. Marysia's family supplied a few dishes, pots, and pans. And so we were settled.

Though I was busy with all these arrangements, I did not forget about the family's jewels buried on the grounds of the factory before we left Kalisz in August of 1939. I was afraid to go near the place immediately. I thought somebody might be spying on me and ready to kill for it. I wanted to wait a little, until life in town became more orderly and, most important, the earth soft enough to dig. Finally we went, Marysia and I.

The two large buildings were the same but everything around them had changed. All the little sheds and the garden were gone. The high wall and the janitor's cottage were gone. Where the garden had been was a new street. The two large buildings had been joined into one big paper factory. The doors were sealed now by the Polish government, and not a soul was in sight.

I was completely disoriented and had no idea where to look for the shed. I thought the place was probably where the street ran now. Marysia and I looked at each other and felt completely helpless. When I look back now, I think I gave up too easily. I was afraid to go to the police and tell them the truth. Who knows what would have happened. I did go to the office whose address was on the document tacked to the doors. I told them who I was, that I was the only survivor of the war, and asked what I could do to get the property back.

They told me that if I could open the factory and start production—paper was badly needed—I could be the manager of the factory. I knew I could not do it alone, but perhaps I could find some of the men who had worked there before the war who knew the machinery, and we could give it a try. I went to a lawyer, an old friend of the family, and told him about it. He advised me against it. He said that all I would have was a big headache. Even if I succeeded in starting the factory, it would eventually be nationalized. But perhaps the government would pay me something for the land and the buildings. I left him my power to represent me and that was the end of my dream of getting some money out of the factory.

I got in touch with a man who had worked for my father

before the war, and worked in the factory for the Germans. I wanted to know if he had heard any rumors of anyone having found the jewelry when they dug for the street construction or took the small buildings away. He was a nice man and I think he would have told me the truth. All he said was that he had not heard a thing about it. He said that for a while the Germans cultivated the garden. It had been such a beautiful place, so quiet, full of flowers and fruit trees right in the middle of a busy city. I would have loved to have some of its fruits and vegetables right then. We certainly needed to save money.

The dream of finding the little jar full of jewelry was gone. I had to do something to earn money.

The sewing courses that I had taken in school in Warsaw came in handy. With the sewing machine I had now, I started my own little business. Nobody had new materials, but everybody had some old clothes that needed to be made longer or shorter, larger or smaller, and I was there to do it. I was on my own and making a living for myself and Marysia.

chapter 20

*A*bout the middle of March, I received a letter from Kazia. She had obtained a permit to move Anek's body to the cemetery.

Marysia did not like the idea of my going to Warsaw. She said they could move Anek without me, but her influence over me was ended. I did what I wanted to do, not what she told me to do. I made enough money to support her and myself. I knew it and she knew it. I really tried to forget and forgive her for the miserable life her behavior had caused for my mother and father. I tried only to remember that she did take me out of the hell. I worked, she cleaned the house and cooked for us, and served somewhat as a companion for me.

The day after I received Kazia's letter, I packed a little bag with a change of clothes and went to Warsaw. Traveling conditions were much better. The trains were now passenger trains—not first-class Pullmans, but much better than the cattle train we had ridden to Kalisz. The train was full of smugglers who were buying food in small villages and taking it to Warsaw, where they sold it at enormous profit. The government tried to prevent this kind of profiteering, but with little success. Warsaw was a major market.

Kazia was very happy to see me. The following day, with all the necessary papers, we went to the cemetery to choose a place for Anek's final rest. In fact, it was not necessary, as we discovered when we arrived. Men worked day and night digging the graves, and as the coffins arrived, they were put in—that was it. There was no such thing as a better or worse place. A whole section of the National Cemetery had been set aside for victims of the uprising. As soon as the box was put in the grave, one man carved the name on the small wooden cross. They had stocks of them ready to be marked.

Another part of the same cemetery was set aside for unidentified coffins and there were many, many of those. In the middle of this section the government had plans to build a mausoleum to the unknown soldier.

When we had all the papers ready, we rented a wooden wagon—a wooden platform on four wheels—and we went to Mokotowska Street. We could see wagons with wooden coffins moving from everywhere toward the cemetery. The government was exhorting the people to do this grim job as fast as possible before the warm weather came. March this year was warm, and we could already smell the odor coming from the shallow graves. With the warm weather, the cleaning of the rubble started full scale and in almost every building people found more bodies, most of the time just a pile of bones.

We hired two men to help dig the grave. We were not sure whether Anek had been buried in a box or just wrapped in cloth, though we suspected that Jan had put the body in a coffin. We had a Polish flag to drape over it.

Some of the graves in the little garden were already

empty. While we were there two other families came for their loved ones. The two men worked quickly though we thought it took hours. When the shovels touched something hard, we breathed a little easier: it was wood. We had both thought about the same thing: what would happen if there was no casket. We would have to pick up the bones.

The men lifted the long wooden box with ropes and set it on the ground. We were so nervous, so shaken, that we did not know what to do first. Kazia wanted to open the box, to be sure that it was Anek. She wanted to see with her own eyes that there was no mistake, that it was her brother in there. She told the men to open the coffin.

The men started to pull at the lid of the box. The rusted nails made noisy squeaks. The wood was almost black and looked partially decomposed. It took them a while to loosen all the nails. Finally the lid came loose but no one had the courage to open the box. Thousands of thoughts swirled in my mind. Maybe it was a mistake, maybe it was not Anek in that box, maybe he was somewhere in a German prison camp. I could smell the freshly turned earth, the odor of decomposing wood, and felt as if I was going to faint. I clutched Kazia's sleeve in order not to fall. In that moment Kazia raised the lid a little. It was Anek, there was no doubt about it. He had on the same suit he had worn when he left home, though the color had changed some—it was darker. His hands were crossed on his chest. They were dark brown and there was no flesh on them. I was afraid to look at his face, but it was covered with a white handkerchief. On one side of him we saw a bottle with a white piece of paper inside. Kazia snatched it and broke it on a piece of stone. The noise was like a shot and the glass scattered everywhere. The wind blew the little piece of paper close to my feet, but I could not bend down to pick it up. I felt as if my arms were made from stone. Somebody picked up the paper and gave it to Kazia. On the paper, in Jan's handwriting, was Anek's name, birth date, the date of his death, and his pseudonym. There was no mistake; it was Anek.

The men closed the box, covered it with the Polish flag, and loaded it onto the wagon. We had not realized that a crowd had gathered around us. Two Russian soldiers stood looking at the box covered with the flag. Somebody took me by the arm and walked me out of the little garden. Kazia and I sat on the side of the wagon and held the box so that it would not slide during the long trip to the cemetery. The horse was trotting fairly fast, the streets were in terrible shape, full of holes from the bombs, and so the trip was far from smooth. When we arrived at the gate of the cemetery, four men lifted the box and carried it to the waiting grave. It happened so fast that Kazia barely had time to pay the men on the wagon. By the time we ran to the graveside, the box was already being lowered into the grave. We threw some earth on top of it and the sound echoed in our hearts. We waited until the grave was covered and the cross put in place. Slowly we walked out of the cemetery. We were the only family there to take Anek to his final rest. Jan was not back from the German camp yet and Rita had nobody to leave the children with.

Two days after the burial I went back to Kalisz.

While I was away, some of our friends had returned to town. Among them were Hania Kerpasz and her mother. Hania had not been my close friend before the war. She was a year younger than I and I had considered her just a baby. But now when we met, we became the best and closest of friends. Hania had lost her father and younger brother. When they came back, her mother obtained an apartment with all the furnishings, rugs, dishes, even personal clothes still in the closets. The Germans had left everything behind. Their apartment was just across the street from mine. They gave me all kinds of clothes and many little things for my home. Every free moment I had I spent across the street with Hania. We spent nights at each other's apartments, and we talked for hours, telling each other of the experiences we had lived through during the war. We talked about all the terrible things that had happened to us, and about the few funny moments.

At the end of April 1945 I found a job as a secretary in the office of a factory that made uniforms for the Russian army. The factory had belonged to friends of my family before the war. Now one of the sons, Arthur Mayor, had returned. The Germans had left all the machinery and a large supply of raw materials. Arthur received a permit to open the factory and direct operations. Before the war they had made ladies' undergarments such as panties, bras, slips, nightgowns. The Germans had done the same things, but in the last weeks they had needed uniforms and that was what Arthur continued to do. Within a few weeks they again started making jersey material and cutting and sewing lingerie. Everything was done under the supervision of the government. All the raw materials came from the government and the manufactured product had to be delivered back to them.

It was my first office job, and I was the only girl in the place. Arthur was a wonderfully understanding boss, who showed me what to do and how to do it. Most of my work was writing production reports, lists of the numbers of pieces made each day. There were no punch clocks, so I had to keep track of how many employees showed up to work each day. I also had the keys to the stockrooms and kept the books. I received all the new merchandise and checked all the cartons that left the factory.

I loved this job. I was so busy all day that I did not have time to think about anything else but what I was doing at that moment. The pay was good. I had enough to take care of Marysia and me. I still added a little to that income by sewing at night. I was home at four, when Marysia had our dinner ready, and after that, depending on how much I had to do, I sat at the sewing machine sometimes until midnight. Often Hania sat with me and helped. It was hard work, but being self-sufficient made me enormously happy. Saturdays and Sundays I had free, and spent them with Hania. We went to the movies or for long walks in the park. The park in Kalisz was one of the most beautiful in Poland. It was divided in the middle by the river Prosna over which there were very picturesque bridges. On both sides the high embankments were edged with tall trees, and in the spring and summer the whole place was planted with flower beds in a profusion of colors.

Not too many of the families we knew came back to Kalisz. Many went abroad to join members of their families. The few that came did not find what they had left behind. Kalisz felt empty. Some of the social organizations had Saturday night get-togethers, but we seldom went.

Toward the end of June, the Boy Scouts held a dance to raise money for their summer camp. Hania and I decided to go. We did not know whether we would meet somebody we knew, but if not we would have something to eat, look around, and go home. We sat at a little table in a corner of the big, bright hall and sipped iced tea and watched all the dancing couples having a good time. We both noticed two very good-looking young men, about our age, one dressed in blue, the other in light gray. They must have been telling jokes to each other. After a few minutes they stopped talking and we knew they had noticed us. They came over and invited us to dance. The one in the gray suit was blond with blue eyes; he invited Hania. The other one, with dark hair and dark-brown eyes, was my partner. They were very polite and introduced themselves as Witold (my partner) and Janusz (Hania's).

Witold was a very good dancer and a very interesting conversationalist. After the first waltz I knew he wanted to finish his education at night school and work during the day. I also learned that Witold lived with his mother and younger brother and had an older sister. It was a very nice evening and for a while we forgot about all our daily troubles.

From that evening on we met almost every day. Sundays the four of us went for long walks. If the weather was good we rented a boat, each of us taking turns rowing. We went as far as the big bridge and a small cafe where we stopped for something cold to drink and to rest for the trip back. These little outings were like a ray of bright sun after the gray everyday routine of hard work. Sometimes during the week we went to the movies or just stayed home and talked. When I had a lot of work to do, all three of them helped me with sewing and then it was fun. Buttons were their specialty. Sometimes they told us all the gossip and news from around town, or we talked about our lives, what we hoped to do. We spoke very seldom about our past.

One day Witold asked me if I would like to have dinner at his home; he wanted me to meet his mother and the rest of his family. "Oh," Hania said, "it looks serious; he wants you to meet his family."

I had a wonderful time. His mother was a very nice lady and his sister was a few years older than I. I thought both of them liked me. His younger brother acted very funny. Every time Witold took my hand the little devil made wisecracks. I guess all this was normal; I found out later that it was the first time Witold had brought a girl friend home. I was honored. His sister, Magda, and I became very good friends. Magda had a little boy about two years old. Her husband had left her before the baby was born. I never asked why and never asked where they had lived during the war. We had known each other for too short a time to become really close, close enough to reveal family secrets.

As the days passed I learned that Witold was a year younger than I. I had thought he was a few years older. He acted so mature and looked much older than seventeen. Age really did not matter, we got along so well. Hania and I, for the first time since the war had ended, felt our own age—two young girls going out with two young men and having a good time.

One warm evening in August, Hania and I sat on our little balcony waiting for Witold and Janusz, but they did not come. One day, two, then a week passed, and they did not come or try to get in touch with us. We had no idea what had happened. At the same time we noticed that a man was following us. We had never seen this man before, and suddenly he was everywhere we went. When I was at home he was always around the entrance to my apartment house. We were frightened. We did not know what was going on, but we suspected a connection between the disappearance of our friends and the man spying on us. We did not go out after dark. Either I slept in Hania's house, or she slept with me. We did not tell anyone about it; we just waited to see what would happen.

During the day I did not have time to think about Witold or the "man on the street." The factory was going full speed. I had to prepare more reports. We did not manufacture as many army uniforms; our production shifted more and more to women's lingerie and we made more of the materials used for it. The knitting machines were on the first floor, the sewing and packing was done on the second floor. My job was to run up and down, get the amounts together, and write the reports. I was glad that my work kept me so busy that I had no time to think about anything else. I had more sewing to do at home as well.

After about two weeks I met Witold on the street. My knees shook and felt like they would cave in and I would fall right there in the middle of the street. Witold touched the tip of his hat as he passed by, and at the same time looked at me with such a sad expression in his eyes that I felt he wanted to tell me something but was afraid to. I met him on the street a few times more and every time he behaved the same way.

August and September passed and nothing changed. The mysterious man still followed us. I feared my own shadow and did not know what to do. Evenings, sometimes until late into the night, I talked with Hania and her mother about our future and came to the conclusion that we did not have much to look forward to in Kalisz. We realized that Russia was gripping Poland tighter and tighter, and the longer we waited the more difficult it would be to get out.

Part of Germany had been incorporated into Poland and the government was encouraging more people to move to this new territory. At the same time people spoke of how easy it was to cross the German and Polish frontiers and reach the American zone in Berlin. From there it would be so much easier to go to faraway places. Many of the people we knew had left Kalisz and we did not hear from them. They had joined members of their families. Hania had a cousin in the U.S.A. I had a great-uncle in New York and an uncle (my father's brother) in Central America. We began to think seriously about going.

Meanwhile I had a week's vacation, and the factory sent me with a few of the other girls to the mountains in the former German territory. It was a beautiful place. A large hotel before the war, it had been turned into a vacation retreat for factory workers. The air was pure, and the hills were covered with pine trees. We walked for miles around the property and were hungry all the time. The food was good and the best part of it was that it cost very little.

When I returned, I told my boss, Arthur, about my plans to go to the West. He thought I was right, but told me if by any chance I was unable to cross the border I could always come back to my job. And if I needed money he could pay me my salary in advance. I thanked him very much and told him that if and when I decided to do it, I would notify him in plenty of time.

Before the war Arthur's family and mine had spent vacations in the same place. One year we had rented the same house. They occupied the downstairs, we had the upstairs. But then the difference in our ages was enormous. Now the seven years meant nothing. Before the war I had just been a crazy kid; now I was a woman.

I think it was when I told him of my plans that Arthur actually saw me as a woman for the first time. From then on he treated me a little differently. He began coming to visit me and invited me to his home. He lived with his mother, an aunt, and her son. I had dinner with them often. I considered him a good and sincere friend, but his mother was terrified that he might be in love with me and, God forbid, marry me. She wanted him to marry a girl with a lot of money, and that certainly was not me. Hania's mother was related in some way to Arthur's aunt, and she told me all about it. Just to irritate and tease the old lady, I openly flirted with Arthur when she was around. But in time I noticed that he looked at me and paid more attention to me at the office. He noticed the way I was dressed, paid me some compliments, and many times when I was working at my desk, I felt he was looking at me.

I decided it was time to make a choice. I was not in love with Arthur and did not plan to stay in Kalisz because of him. I never talked about my plans with Marysia. I was afraid she would do something to prevent me from going. She had ample reason to do so; I was her meal ticket. She had a home and a reasonably good life. She cooked and kept house for the two of us and that left her plenty of time to run around with her old cronies and gossip. I was sure she would do everything possible to prevent me from leaving.

Though we did not fight, my nerves were on edge, because when I was at home she would not leave me alone. Even when I had company it seemed she was always near me. I think she loved me in her own strange way. She had worked for my grandmother even before I was born, she had watched me grow up, and until now had tried to tell me what to do and how to do it. Sometimes I let her think that she was the "boss" just to have peace, but more and more I let her know that I was grown up enough to make my own decisions. Finally I asked her not to stay in the room when I had company. She did not like that at all; her dark brown eyes flashed with anger, but she did not say a word.

Marysia could not read or write and she thought that any letter I wrote was a criticism of her. In fact, the only letters I wrote were to Kazia in Warsaw and she knew Marysia well enough that I did not have to write about her. Marysia's family lived in Kalisz; she had a brother, two nieces, and a cousin with a large family. Her brother and one of his daughters were the only ones she got along with. They both came to the apartment often and she helped them as much as she could. I made Jadwiga some dresses; the poor girl had nothing to wear and her father drank all the money he earned.

I did not know whether Marysia helped them with money. She told me that she had none of my grandmother's jewelry or gold pieces left. I was not sure I could believe her. I did not need the money now; I earned more than enough for both of us. If she had something left, she was welcome to keep it. In fact, I hoped she did have some pieces hidden away; if my plans materialized, she would need some money to hold her until I could send her help.

We finally decided, Hania, her mother, and I, to try our voyage into the unknown. Hania and her mother sold what they could from their apartment. I could not touch a thing without Marysia knowing it and that was the last thing I wanted to do.

We obtained all the papers necessary to move to the new territory. We decided to go to Szczecin, a port on the river Odra. We had heard that it was easier to find a guide to cross the Polish-German border there. We planned to leave about a week before Christmas, exactly the fifteenth of December.

chapter 21

*I*n the beginning of December
I told Arthur about our trip.
He looked sad. Lately we had seen more and more of each
other after work and I was sure he would miss me. Until now
I had been certain he was not serious about our relationship.
To me it was a friendship. I was flattered by his attentions.
He was very attentive but not very romantic. He started to
kiss me good night, but it was a kiss on the cheek. Then
during the last week he did find where my lips were. It was a
surprise to me; I realized then that he thought of me as more
than just a friend. We had a long talk that evening. I told him
frankly that I thought we were just good friends. He smiled
and told me that the feeling of just friendship had ended some
time ago—for him anyway. He said he would like very much
for me to stay, but could not ask me to marry him right now.

The situation in the factory was very uncertain, his job there shaky. They were going to nationalize all the factories and they would not keep the past owners as directors. Suddenly I looked at him not as a friend and a boss but as a man, a very good-looking man, tall, slim, with a head full of dark-brown hair and very big and expressive dark eyes. No, I did not want to even think of becoming romantically involved. My mind was made up. I was going and nothing would stop me. Then I almost started to laugh, thinking of what his mother would do if she could see him now.

I told Marysia that I was going with Hania for a two-week winter vacation. I packed a knapsack with two changes of underwear, two dresses, an extra pair of shoes, and a sweater. I left everything in the apartment, and when I closed the door behind me I was not sad or sorry. I left everything that I had bought with my own hard-earned money. I was leaving a life I knew to go into an unknown future. But I wanted to be with my family, the very little that was left of it.

How Witold learned that I was leaving—the exact day and time—I don't know. He came to the railroad station and stayed there with me until the train left, which was four hours later. He begged me to forgive him. He told me he wanted to talk me into staying but had no right to do so. He said that I was the only girl he had ever loved and he would join me in Berlin (he knew exactly where we were going). He said that in his first letter he would write me what had happened. He would tell me everything that he could not tell me now.

Just seeing him at the station shook me. I knew there was some kind of mystery behind his behavior, and I still cared for him. I hesitated for a moment. Maybe I should stay with the familiar and not reach for something new. But at that moment we heard the whistle of the train. I had no time to think any longer about changing my decision. I was going! The train stopped and Hania half pushed me in. At the second whistle the train started to move.

Witold kept one promise; he did write to me—long, long

letters for about two years after I left Kalisz. But he never wrote one word about what had happened, and why he so suddenly stopped seeing me. Maybe the letters were censored. I don't know.

The trip to Szczecin went well. I cried a little and Hania tried to cheer me. I was not crying because I had left Kalisz behind but because I was afraid to lead a homeless life again for who knew how long.

In Poznan we waited about four hours for our train and the next day we arrived in Szczecin. The city government gave us a small room in the special quarters for new settlers. We left our few pieces of luggage in the room and went out to learn what our chances were for getting to Berlin. We had to be very careful; the city was full of thieves and police. By lucky chance, Mrs. Kerpasz, Hania's mother, met an old acquaintance on the street, old Mr. Perleski and his son Sam. The old man knew everything about everything. He put together all the information and told us that the best way was to go to Wroclaw and cross the border there. He gave us the address of someone who could help us.

The next day we packed our knapsacks again and took a train to Wroclaw. The city was in ruins, with no electricity, and it was very difficult to find a place to stay for the night. It was the middle of December and cold and windy. We walked the streets and asked everybody we met if they knew where we could find rooms.

We needed two rooms because Mr. Perleski and his son had traveled with us to Wroclaw and we wanted to stay together. It was safer to travel with the two men. Finally we met a woman who gave us an address where, she thought, there was a place available. We did get two rooms. There was one bed in each room and a broken stove.

The following morning Mrs. Kerpasz and Mr. Perleski left early to learn whether and how soon we might leave for Berlin. They returned late in the day with some good news. They had talked to a man who led one of the border crossing operations. He knew the guides and the soldiers that helped them and required the money in advance. He gave Mrs. Kerpasz the address where we were to wait for the truck and described what make and color it would be. From that moment on we would be on our own; he was not responsible for whatever happened once we were in the truck. The next transport was scheduled for the twenty-fourth of December, 1945. It was hoped that during the Christmas holidays, the control would be eased. Mr. Perleski and his son were to take another truck. He told us that if everything went well, we would meet in Berlin; but he did not say where.

Just as the man had told us, the big truck appeared at the prearranged place and time on the twenty-fourth. It was a big transport truck, covered with heavy canvas. As soon as it stopped, two soldiers jumped out, picked us up, put us in the truck, and told us to sit at the far end. Then they covered us and filled the truck with hay. They told us that as soon as we had left the city we could change position and cover ourselves with blankets but that we should at no point get out from under the hay. They also told us that when the truck stopped it would probably be at the border. They could not permit the guards to check inside the truck, so there might be some shooting, and we were to lie flat then and make no noise.

That was the only time we saw our guides. The truck did stop at the border, but there was no shooting. The truck was not inspected, so we just moved on.

I did not know how long we rode—I probably fell asleep —but finally the truck stopped again. We peeked out from under the hay. It was very dark; we had no idea where we were. Then we heard the driver shouting at us to get off, that we were in Berlin and this was as far as they would take us. They waited long enough for us to jump off with our little knapsacks and then they were gone. We were left standing on the dark, empty street in an unknown city with no place to go. For a moment we were not sure whether we were actually in Berlin. They could have left us in any city, on any corner, and we would not have known the difference. The three of us felt completely lost.

We picked up our knapsacks and suitcases and started to walk, just to move forward. Presently we saw what looked like a small hotel. From outside it looked dark and empty, but a small sign at one side of the door, "Hotel," encouraged us to walk in. The night clerk was sleeping at his desk in the dingy lobby. He jumped up, startled, when we entered. He explained to us that Berlin had a curfew; after 8 P.M. nobody could be seen on the streets of the Russian zone. Oh, we had landed in the Russian part of Berlin. Mrs. Kerpasz was the only one among us who spoke some German. She explained to the clerk that we had just arrived and did not know about the curfew hour, that we wanted a room only for one day, and that tomorrow we could travel home. The clerk told us he would give us the room tonight, but tomorrow we would have to register at the Russian command post. Mrs. Kerpasz smiled nicely and said, of course we would do that.

Our room had one big bed, a little table, two chairs, and a wardrobe. It was almost as cold as outside; one glass panel in the window was missing. We were so tired and frightened that we went to bed fully dressed and covered ourselves with one wonderful thing the room had—a big, thick goosedown comforter. We all fell asleep immediately; nothing could keep us awake, neither the cold nor worry about what tomorrow would bring.

Suddenly we were awakened by a pounding at the door. We stiffened with fright, but had to open the door. Hania was the brave one. She opened the door just a little. Two Russian military policemen were at the door, checking on who was in the room. We were terrified; they could take us to jail and send us back to Poland. We did not know what they were going to do with us.

They looked around for a moment and told us they were looking for deserters from the army; they were not interested in civilians. But they suddenly became interested in two young girls, like Hania and me. They started asking questions— where were we from and where were we going? Hania told them very quickly that we had worked in Germany on a farm during the war and now we were on the way home to Poland, and she just closed the door right in their faces.

During this conversation I had slipped under the covers and almost stopped breathing. If they had stayed a little longer I might have suffocated. Hania really had courage. We waited to hear another knock at the door—maybe they would shoot off the lock and run in and rape us—but they turned around and left. We could hear their steps fading away.

Of course after that visit we could not sleep any more. As soon as it was late enough not to look suspicious, Mrs. Kerpasz paid for the room and we left quietly, heading for the American zone.

chapter **22**

*B*erlin was divided into four
zones, American, English,
French, and Russian, but at this time people could move
freely from one part to another. We knew that in the American
zone we could stay in a DP (displaced persons) camp. They
had been set up by charitable organizations and gave shelter
and food to people who preferred staying in Germany and
waiting for visas to the U.S.A. rather than going back home
to Eastern Europe. Most of them knew that their families had
not survived, and some, like us, arrived after the war was
over.

After walking for what we felt were hours, we saw on
the corner of the next street a sign: ENTERING AMERICAN ZONE.
We almost ran to it and when we had passed it, we just
looked at each other: we had made it!

But we did not know where the camp was. I looked at the people passing by—whom to ask for directions? We picked one man who looked like a DP. Displaced persons had a certain appearance—poorly dressed, pale, with a hunted look—but it seemed that everyone in Berlin looked like that. The man we asked did not speak Polish, but understood what we wanted. He told us, half in German, half in English, but we were unable to understand his directions. We tried our luck three more times and finally we found our man. He advised us to go first to the registration office and they would send us to the proper place. We did just that and were assigned to the DP camp in Schlachtensee.

Schlachtensee was a German military camp, situated in a pleasant residential district of Berlin that had suffered very little from bombing. Now it served as a home for people who had been liberated from concentration camps or labor camps —people who did not want to return to the East, but preferred to wait there for a visa to the U.S.A., Palestine, or any free country that would accept them.

The camp was run by UNRRA, the United Nations Relief and Rehabilitation Administration, an organization with only one goal: to help people who had survived the hell of this war.

We were given a small room with two beds (I slept with Hania in one, her mother in the other), a table and two chairs, and a small wardrobe. The room was clean, the beds narrow but with clean sheets and blankets. We were assigned hours for eating our breakfast, lunch, and dinner. The portions were large but the food did not have much taste. Many people complained continually, but Hania and I were happy with what we received. How could I complain? I had a place to live and plenty of food because people in America had donated the money for it. I even received a ration of cigarettes. I did not smoke, but cigarettes came in very handy if I wanted to buy something outside the camp; they were better than money.

A few days after we had settled in the camp, I wrote a

letter to Marysia. I tried to explain to her why I had done what I did. I told her that I did not see a future for myself in Kalisz, that what I had done was very risky, but I had to take that chance. I told her that wherever I was, I would help her with whatever I had, that the apartment and the furniture were hers and she could do with them what she wished. (I found out years later that she gave everything to her niece, and that she still had some gold pieces and kept them until her death. For years I sent her things that she asked for, things that could be sold easily, like nylons, knitting wool, and clothes. When she died her room was full of packages from me, some not even opened.)

Life in the camp was monotonous, but we could come and go as we pleased. Hania and I walked around the city, looking at the ruins of all the famous places like the Brandenburg Gate and Hitler's government buildings. We went to the movies, and for our cigarettes we could buy anything we wanted to eat. The Germans would do anything and everything for a cigarette. For ten cigarettes I had my hair washed and set and for a whole pack I could get a dress or a pair of shoes. Hania smoked her allotment; her mother and I saved ours. Hania really smoked too much and it caused friction between her and her mother. I told her the same thing, but we never quarreled. When she finished her pack, she knew she could have mine. We were like sisters, but closer. We not only loved each other, we had the same likes and dislikes. We spent all our time together, and never grew bored with each other's company. Though Hania was a year younger than I, she was taller and stronger and treated me like a little sister. We had no secrets from one another.

At that time all the girls in the camp coveted a job at Chaplain Shubow's place. He was an American army chaplain and had charge of a large house not far from the camp, where he distributed clothes and food packages to the needy. American charity organizations sent things to him and his staff unpacked all the donations and redistributed them.

He had a couple as housekeepers, Mr. and Mrs. Lubski,

and three girls who helped in the storage room. There were also two German women who cleaned and cooked. Everybody agreed that Mrs. Lubski was a very energetic and self-sufficient woman. Some thought she was just wonderful, that she worked very hard to help as many people as possible, that she was very kind to the needy and went out of her way to please everybody. Then there were others who said that she acted like a queen and gave the best things to the people she knew. I did not pay much attention to all this talk. I had never been to her house and never asked for help from Chaplain Shubow. Later I realized that in her position one just can't please the whole world. People were seldom satisfied with what they received. They blamed Mr. Lubski if they found a dirty or torn piece of clothing in their package. Everything that came from the U.S.A., new and old, was distributed to the people in the camp, but they were never satisfied. Mrs. Lubski could have been an angel, and they would still have found fault.

One day the secretary in the camp office told me that Mrs. Lubski wanted to see me. Hania and I went right over to Zehlendorf, the section of Berlin where Chaplain Shubow's home and office was. It was not far from the camp. After two stops by U-bahn (Berlin subway) and four blocks of walking we were standing in front of a beautiful two-story villa with a garden around it and an American flag fluttering on the roof. My heart beat faster; it was the first time that I had stood so close to the American flag. Perhaps I would be lucky enough to see the whole country soon. That was a main topic of conversation in the camp: where and when we would go to the States. How beautiful it was, how people there were free to do what they wanted and buy whatever they wished.

The gate and the front door were open. We found this strange because we were so used to closed doors. We asked for Mrs. Lubski in the front office. In less than a minute she appeared. She told me that her husband was from Kalisz, that both of them knew my family, and that she had just heard that "little Lilly" was in the Schlachtensee camp. She gave

Hania and me two big food packages and told us that if we lacked clothing, we could get as much as we needed. She asked me if I would have time to come every day and take care of her little son. She had so much to do in the office— there were more and more packages coming in and more to be given away—that she just did not have time for her baby. Little Joe was two years old, and like any active boy, had to be watched every minute.

I had all the time in the world, so I accepted the job. I did not know what to say, but I was thrilled.

Now I was a working girl. I left the camp at 9 A.M. and came back at about 6 P.M. Often Hania came to the house early and we ate dinner together and went back to the camp together. This life was like a dream; it reminded me a little of my life before the war. I spent my days in a warm, clean house, far from the little scuffles in the camp and the tasteless food from the big kettles.

The house was large and beautifully furnished. On the first floor was a small room, which was the chaplain's private office, and a large room, where he received people who needed help. In the evening this room served for dining when he had company. Next to it were a good-sized kitchen and storage rooms. On the second floor Mr. and Mrs. Lubski had two rooms, the girls had two smaller rooms, the chaplain had a bedroom, and any small nook was used as storage space. The whole basement was a sorting place, where all the packages from the States were received and opened.

My life started to have some meaning to me. I spent the day with little Joe. I dressed him, fed him, read him all kinds of stories, and when the weather was nice took him for a walk. In the beginning he was not enthusiastic about me. He cried when his mother left the room, and I was not a very patient nanny, but after a few days he grew used to me and we had a wonderful time together. I ate what everyone else in the house did. I had not seen so many luxury items since before the war. We had chocolate, dried fruit, juices, and fresh fruit. I took whatever I could to the camp for Hania and her mother, and Mrs. Lubski often gave me packages to take "home."

Besides taking care of the baby I helped with chores around the house. When company was expected for dinner, I helped to set the table. Sometimes Mrs. Lubski gave me the keys to the pantry to give the cook what she needed for that day. When they were very busy in the basement, I lent a helping hand there.

In the middle of March I received a document from the Polish consulate in Berlin requesting to see me. I did not want to go by myself and took Hania with me. One of the secretaries, a very nice lady, told me that the Swiss consulate in Warsaw had a transit visa for me and all the necessary papers for my passage to El Salvador. She told me that the best course for me would be to go back to Poland. It was easy, because they were sending transports back to Poland from all over Germany, with the Polish government paying for it. I thanked her and told her that I would decide very soon and contact her again.

Now I knew that my family in El Salvador wanted me to come there. My uncle, my father's brother, who had lived there for many years, had left Poland before I was born. The only time I had seen him was when he came to Poland in the summer of 1933, met my mother's cousin and, after a very short courtship, married her. The wedding had been the most exciting event in our family in a long time. During World War I my father's family had lived in Switzerland. My father was studying to be an engineer and his brother was in medical school in France. When the rest of the family returned to Poland, Wladek had stayed in France and from there had gone to Central America to seek adventure and a new life in a new continent. During the war, as long as it was possible, they had sent us small packages through the International Red Cross, but once the ghetto was closed, we no longer heard from them. Now they had discovered that I had survived—perhaps through the Red Cross or through the government in Kalisz.

When I returned from the Polish consulate, I asked everyone for advice. Nearly everyone was against my going back to Poland. Mr. and Mrs. Lubski promised to ask the chaplain about it. He had answers to every problem and this time he had a good idea. One of the officers, a journalist who was very often a guest in "our house," was going to Warsaw on official business. The chaplain's idea was for George to go to the Swiss consulate there and get all the papers or arrange for the Swiss consul to send them to the American consulate in Berlin. The Swiss did not have a representative in Berlin yet. I was happy to find somebody I could trust. All I could do now was wait. He was scheduled to return in early April.

For some time now, there had been rumors in the camp about the Americans wanting to send as many people as possible to the camps in West Germany. The largest was in Munich. Berlin was just a little island surrounded by the Russians. The situation did not look good. We had heard about arrests in the Russian zone. When I went out with Hania we paid close attention to where we were going and tried to avoid the Russian zone. We then heard that the Russians had arrested two American soldiers, and from that point on the situation became more tense. On the streets that formed the borders between the zones, the Americans put up large signs saying, "Here ends American protectorate." France and England did the same. People could still pass from one zone to the other without hindrance, however.

When people talk about something, it always happens eventually. In the first days of April the move began. Originally they wanted to send only people who wished to go to Munich, but there were so many that the first to go were the old and the very young and the largest families.

Hania and her mother did not feel safe in Berlin; they thought that from Munich it would be easier to get to the States. Conditions in Munich were much better and people were worried that the Russians would eventually take over the whole city of Berlin. Hania stayed with me and her mother went alone. Hania wanted to wait to see what would happen with my papers, if and when they came.

After about ten days, when there was still no news of George's return, Hania decided to go to Munich to join her mother. She did not want to leave her alone for too long. The situation was very uncertain and she was worried that they would be separated for a long time.

When we said good-bye in Berlin, neither I nor Hania thought for a moment that it would be seven long years before we saw each other again. We expected that in a week, or at the most two weeks, I would join them in Munich.

The day Hania left I moved with all my belongings— one small knapsack—to the chaplain's house. Recently one of the girls who helped Mrs. Lubski had married an American officer and her place was vacant. I shared a luxurious room with a girl my age. I no longer took care of little Joe during the day, but I still watched him in the evenings or on special occasions. Most of my time was spent in the basement sorting the packages and taking care of the people in need. Mrs. Lubski trusted me completely and left me all the keys to the storage rooms when she went out. The place was always busy with people coming and going. New people from the camp came for clothes; some had arrived in Berlin with just what they had on their backs. We tried to help everybody. Many soldiers and officers, American, English, and French, were looking for relatives in Poland. They often had lists of people they were trying to locate for friends at home. We worked closely with the camp in Schlachtensee and with the Red Cross.

We did not have so-called office hours; Chaplain Shubow's house was open all the time for people in need. I was in a place that was doing something to help people, a place where things were happening. I was in touch with Americans and I could put to use the little English I knew; every day I grew a little better at it. The Americans I met were the nicest, best-looking men—or was it my imagination? No, it was not my imagination; they were so helpful, so polite, so attentive. It was a tiny bit of America that I was living in, and I loved it. My imagination and my dreams ran wild. Was it possible that one day I would live in this dream country?

I worked long, hard hours, and I was gaining weight. I worked all day and I ate all day. I loved sweets and spaghetti in tomato sauce. I could eat spaghetti three times a day. We had cases of spaghetti with meat balls, in tomato sauce, in cheese sauce, and I think I ate a large part of the supply. The cook prepared all the meals for the people living in the house but there were always twice that many when the meals were served; whoever was in the office at that time was invited to stay.

I was glad that Mrs. Lubski kept me busy. The one day a week I had free I stayed home. I missed Hania very much. We were used to going out together and being together all the time. I did not feel like going to the movies or eating out or taking a long walk by myself. We had taken great pleasure in little things that happened during our stay in Germany. For instance, we did not have to stand in line to get into the movies; the lines were for the Germans—we just went to the cashier and bought tickets. My "uniform" helped considerably. The girls who worked at the chaplain's wore navy blue skirts, light blue blouses, and navy blue caps just like those of the American soldiers. It was not really an American uniform, but it looked important and the Germans did not know any better—in those early days anyway. When we looked at those long lines of Germans waiting not only to go to the movies but to buy food, we thought of how many of them had been Gestapo or SS men. Now they looked frightened. For one or two of our cigarettes they would even shine our shoes with their own shirts.

At night before I fell asleep, I thought about the little things that had happened to Hania and me, some of them funny. Going home from one of our last outings together, we took the U-Bahn. In the seats in front of us were two American soldiers. One of them was a particularly ugly young man. He had red hair, a face full of freckles, and big, floppy ears. We looked at him and then at each other and began talking about his looks.

"Look at this tall carrot sitting across from us," I said.

"Look at those freckles; he must have taken a sunbath with a colander over his face," Hania said.

"Oh, look at those big ears; he would kill us if he knew what we're talking about," I said. We talked about his face, his hands, his feet. The poor fellow did not have a stitch on him that we did not criticize. After a few stops the two soldiers got up, ready to leave, and the redheaded one turned toward us and said in fluent Polish, "Good-bye, ladies, until we meet again."

We looked at each other and could not believe our ears. The blood drained from our faces and then we felt our cheeks flush. We wanted to say something to him, apologize, tell him that we had done it for fun, but the two men were gone. From the platform, as our train started to move, they waved to us and blew us a kiss. I think the redhead actually was not angry; he seemed amused at our reaction when we realized that he had understood all our remarks. We never, never again talked about people in any language. That was a good lesson.

Every free moment I had, I thought about Hania and her mother. What were they doing in Munich, what were the living conditions like there? I wanted to join them, but had not yet heard about my papers.

Meanwhile the American consulate opened in Berlin and started to process affidavits sent from families in the States. Charitable organizations were also sending affidavits to people who had no families anywhere. Every country had a quota and those who had come first to Berlin had a better chance of leaving first. The only problem was that there were so many people from Poland that a large proportion of them would have to wait much longer.

Mr. and Mrs. Lubski and little Joe had all their papers ready so that they could leave on the first ship sailing from Bremen to America. At about the same time Chaplain

Shubow's tour of duty in Germany was ending. He, of course, could go back on any military transport, but decided to wait and go with all the DPs—most of them people whom he had helped for so long, and many of whom he knew by their first names.

It was a sad day when the Lubski family and the chaplain left. We all went to the train station. Many had flowers for the chaplain and all of us cried.

Chaplain Friedman came to replace Chaplain Shubow. He was a much younger man, a doctor of philosophy from the state of Colorado, and as kind and helpful as his predecessor.

Early in June one of the girls working with me married an American officer and she left at the same time as Chaplain Shubow and the Lubskis. I still did not have news from "my friend George" or the papers from Poland. And now I had more responsibility and more work. I was one of the "old" helping hands, who knew where everything was, and how to run this large, busy household. Chaplain Friedman promised to find a couple to take Mr. and Mrs. Lubski's place and after about two weeks Mr. and Mrs. Berman arrived. They were older than the Lubskis and to me they seemed my parents' age.

I gave Mrs. Berman all the keys, showed her where everything was, and hoped for the best. She was a pleasant lady, not as aggressive and officious as Mrs. Lubski, but she fit into her new role as head of the household very well. We worked together, helping each other, and got along beautifully.

Flowers were in full bloom—it was summer in Berlin. The garden in the back of the house looked wonderful. As often as I could I joined the young people sitting under the big cherry tree. The fruit was ripe, and the soldiers, some of whom visited us daily, climbed the tree, picked the ripe cherries, and threw them down to us. They were delicious, sweet and juicy.

June was almost over and I still did not know what had happened to my papers. I knew that the consulate was preparing the second transport to America. Finally I decided to talk with Chaplain Friedman about it. After work he often joined us in the garden and I waited for the right moment to talk to him about my problem. But there were too many people around him. Usually the young soldiers and officers sang, or carried on discussions, or just had fun eating and drinking Cokes. I finally caught him in his office alone, explained to him about George, that he still had not come back, and that I truly did not know what to do.

"Why are you so stubbornly waiting for those papers?" he asked me.

"What can I do?" I asked. "I don't want to go back to Poland for those papers. I thought it was a wonderful opportunity when George offered to bring them back. But it has been so long, I just don't know what has happened to him."

"Do you have any family in the U.S.A.?" he asked me.

"Yes, I know my great-uncle [my grandmother's brother] lives in New York, but I don't have his address," I answered.

"Do not worry about that," the Chaplain said, "the consulate will find out. We will go there tomorrow and we will see what they can do for you."

He told me not to say anything about my uncle in Central America, because there were no other consulates in Berlin besides the American and that would just complicate my chances for leaving Berlin on the next transport.

Next transport—I could not believe what I had heard him say. He did not mean that. How was it possible?

The next day we drove to the American consulate. (It was an experience—one in a lifetime—to ride in a jeep with an American flag blowing in the breeze. I felt like a queen.) I waited for a short time while Chaplain Friedman talked to the consul in his office. He came out, all smiles, and presented me to the consul. Looking at his smiling face I knew he was happy with whatever they had spoken about. He had told the consul that I had been working in his office, that I was a great help to him, but that he would like me to go to the States as soon as it could be arranged. The consul took me to one of his assistants, who asked me a thousand questions. On the way back I thanked Chaplain Friedman for all the troubles and time he had taken to help me. He was happy with the interview and told me that very soon he would have to say good-bye to me. He would have to look for somebody to take my place. He said I had done a wonderful job and it would be difficult to replace me. I almost cried.

A few days later I received a note from the consulate asking me to come in for passport pictures within the next two days.

When I arrived, one clerk took my pictures, another gave me some papers to fill out, and a third took me to the doctor's office. The doctor gave me a checkup, and a nurse took some of my blood for testing. Then they told me to go home and wait for further instructions.

I did not feel well when I got home; I felt weak and dizzy. Maybe they had taken too much of my blood. Mrs. Berman ordered me to bed and gave me two big glasses of tomato juice, which was supposed to be good for replacing blood cells. I think it was nerves. Had the tests turned out right? Would they find my great-uncle in New York?

I waited every day for the letter with the stamp of the U.S. consulate, and when it came a few days later, I was afraid to open it. Many people had been through all the preliminary procedures only to receive a letter informing them that they would have to wait, for one reason or another. I opened the letter. I could not believe my eyes: the consul informed me that I had been issued a visa to enter the United States of America, and that all I had to do was go to the consulate to sign some more papers. I was there within the hour.

I had to sign a great stack of papers, and then they took my fingerprints—all ten of them. I had to swear that all I had told them was true. The consul shook my hand and told me I was ready to leave on the next transport.

I could not believe all that happened in the next few days. I had waited for this moment for so long and now could not comprehend that it was here. I did not even have time to write to Hania. I was sorry now that they had gone to Munich. If they had stayed in Berlin I was sure Chaplain Friedman would have helped them as well. As it turned out, if I had not been waiting for the papers from Poland, I would have gone with them and would have had to wait for the visa probably as long as they did, which was three years.

When I returned home everybody came to congratulate me and wanted to know to the smallest detail what I had been asked, what I had to do, what I had had to sign. The next transport was leaving on the second of July. I had two weeks to get ready.

The chaplain told me to choose a package for myself— some nice dresses and everything I might need for the trip and for some time afterward. Now as I unpacked and sorted the things in the basement, I looked for dresses, shoes, and underwear that would fit me. I was so excited I really did not know what I was doing. I found a winter coat that I thought was the most beautiful thing I had ever seen. It was made from brown imitation fur with kelly green trimming; it was brand new and I did not even have to shorten it. (This coat traveled with me from Berlin to the U.S.A. and from there to Central America. In the tropical climate there I never wore it, but kept it . . . and kept it. When I used it on my trip to the States seven years later, it was called a "displaced person's" coat by my family. Finally when I sent it with other clothes to Poland, it still looked new.)

The second of July came. The chaplain took me to the station, where we joined the other people going to Bremen to meet the ship—the second transport carrying DPs to America. Everyone from the house came to the station to say good-bye. I was a little sad, just a little, to leave these good friends behind, but I was too excited to think about what the future might have in store for me. The others were sad to see me go. We had spent so much time together and we were so used to living together, but we all knew that that was just temporary. Chaplain Shubow had left, the Lubskis had left, and now it was my turn.

We had heard stories about the first ship's arrival in the United States. It had been met by a large fleet of boats in New York harbor and had sailed into the harbor with fireboats putting on a water show, sirens blasting in the city, and a group of dignitaries waiting at the dock. I wondered if our second transport would receive the same welcome—I doubted that such fantastic stories could be true.

Riding in the car to the station, I kept closing my eyes. I could not believe that I would be on this second transport. My thoughts jumped from one thing to another. I had waited for this moment for so long, but right now it seemed to me that everything was moving too fast.

There were not very many people waiting for the train; we were to meet the rest in the port of Bremen. Then it was time to go. I embraced the chaplain, kissed him, thanked him for all he had done for me, and kissed Mr. and Mrs. Berman. It was like a dream; I was in the train and the train was slowly moving. From the window I could see my friends waving white handkerchiefs; then the train moved faster and the people grew smaller and smaller until they looked like little specks. Then the station disappeared.

I sat in the corner with watery eyes. I did not know whether I was crying because I had left so many nice people behind or from happiness at going to America.

I had no idea what to expect. I knew that my family in El Salvador had cared enough to secure papers for me to go and live with them. I knew I had somebody who wanted to help me. Even though I never had received all the papers from Poland, I knew that from the United States it would be much easier to get in touch with my uncle in El Salvador. During my last visit to the American consul in Berlin, he had told me that they had reached my great-uncle in New York and that he would be waiting for me at the pier. Then I worried about whether I would be able to recognize him. He had lived in London for many years, but moved to New York just before the war. I only remembered him from the pictures. I had been too young the one time he was in Kalisz to remember him, whereas I remembered my uncle from El

Salvador very well and his wife even better. Before her marriage we had been together all the time. Many years had passed since then. I had grown from a little, protected, and slightly spoiled girl into an "old" woman; not old in years but very old in experience. I was hoping to find a home and a family; I was hoping my lonely and sad life was over. I was going to the land of my dreams—what more could I ask?

The people on the train were noisy, happy to leave Berlin behind. They were singing, telling each other their plans for tomorrow. Everybody had hopes for a better tomorrow.

chapter 23

*I*n Bremen empty quarters awaited us. Before we entered the building two nurses sprayed everybody with some powder that was supposed to kill any "bugs" we had on us. They checked every name against their list and gave everybody a number. That number was our only document and that number was our permit to enter the U.S.A.

After that we were assigned our room numbers and our bed numbers. We were living in school buildings. The rooms were large with a row of beds along each wall. The beds were very clean and the food very tasty. It did not bother me that I had to sleep in the same room with all these strange people. It would only be a few days. I met some girls my age and we became friends. They were all orphans, going to a home, and there they would stay until somebody adopted them.

It made me very sad to think about them, going so far to a strange country, without hope of finding a relative. They were such a nice group of girls, I hoped they would find good, loving families. I thought my future looked so much brighter. I was thankful to God, grateful for helping me to survive and guiding me.

All the buildings were surrounded by barbed wire. There was only one entrance, guarded at all times by two American MPs. We could move freely in and out of the buildings, but no strangers could get in. Bremen had suffered a lot during the war, and there was not much to look at. The houses near our camp were pleasant, with good-sized gardens. For a few cigarettes the German housewives gave us all the fruit we wanted. We had cherries, gooseberries, and raspberries. We had nothing to do but wait, so we sat on the grass in the sun and ate the fruit while talking about the trip and the wonderful future that awaited us.

On July 12, 1946, we were transported to the ship. They checked numbers again and then slowly, one by one, we walked across the gangplank onto the deck. The ship, the *Marine Flasher*, was an army transport, but to me it looked like a luxury liner. The officer on the deck gave me the number of my cabin, and the number of my bed. Another man helped me with the luggage and took me to my cabin. The cabins were large and the bunk beds were three-tiered. Mine was the one in the middle. I did not mind that. The only trouble I found later was that my neighbors above and below were both seasick the whole time, and sometimes kept me awake.

Once all the people had been checked in, the ship moved slowly away from the pier. After a while the buildings of Bremen faded away, Germany faded away, and the whole of Europe faded away. I hoped all my terrible memories would fade away as well.

The first two days on the ship were very interesting. I walked the length and width of it, asking endless questions. I was one of the few on deck; many were seasick, even though the sea seemed calm and the ship glided over the waves very smoothly. The food was good; I am sure a great deal of the trouble of the sick passengers was due to over-eating. It was the first time since the beginning of the war that I had been served oranges. I had almost forgotten how they tasted. The ice cream was the best I had ever eaten. I spent a lot of time on deck; the fresh sea breeze gave me an enormous appetite. We had nothing to do; everything was done for us. That was something I was not used to, but could grow accustomed to quickly.

On the third day of the trip the sky suddenly darkened. The voice of the captain came over the loudspeakers. He told us that we were approaching a severe storm and to be careful not to go on deck. He really did not have to say that. The moment the ship started to rock from side to side most of the people ran to their cabins and stayed in bed, some of them sick, some of them just frightened.

The storm was indeed severe. Outside the portholes the ocean was almost black. From one moment to another it seemed like enormous holes opened in the water and that they would swallow our little ship. It rocked quite violently, not only from side to side, but up and down. The bow looked like it was touching the sky one moment and then dipped down and touched the water the next. That night there were only two persons in the dining room—I was one of them. I did not get seasick at all, but I was afraid to go to the cabin. When it grew late, I became very tired and decided finally to go downstairs. I felt so sleepy that I thought nothing would bother me. I was almost right—the noises of sick people did not bother me that much, but the smell was terrible. The girl in the bottom bunk was so sick she thought she would die. She begged me to find a doctor or the nurse; perhaps they could give her some medication. It took me a while to find the nurse, and she gave me a pill that she said should help a little. There was not much they could do for that kind of sickness. By the time I got back I was so tired that nothing kept me from falling asleep.

The next day when we awoke, the weather was beautiful, the sea calm, and the sun shining, but the sick people were too weak to enjoy it.

On the seventh day of our voyage I saw the Statue of Liberty far away in the early morning mist. It was cool and very windy but everybody came on deck. I was shaking—I'm not certain if it was from the cold or because it was so overwhelming for me to see the Statue of Liberty, the symbol of all my dreams. Now that it was drawing nearer and nearer, I felt like I could almost touch it. As the ship moved forward I could see the contours of the tall buildings. They looked like big blocks of black granite, but in my imagination they were fairy-tale castles.

As we drew closer and closer I could see the neon signs and the lights in the windows in these unbelievably tall buildings.

I started to cry. I just could not stop, but this time the tears were from happiness. I had made it. The country of my dreams was right in front of me. I could almost touch it. I felt the salty taste of my own tears and thought that I should not cry now. What I had lived through was a terrible nightmare and I would never forget it, but now in front of me was a new life. We were now passing very close to the Statue of Liberty. I looked up and felt as though the Lady was looking at me and smiling. It would be a happy life: that was my destiny.

EPILOGUE

*D*ear Readers, in the beginning of the book I thanked the people who were part of my life before I started to write. Now I would like to add the most important thank you's, to the people who are part of my life now.

I am grateful to my husband of twenty-seven years, Bernard Shepard, whom I met in El Salvador, for his understanding during the months I was translating this book. A host of memories came back to me then and I was not a very understanding companion and mother. The dining-room table was full of papers and a clicking typewriter, leaving no place to eat or for our daughter Susan to do homework. Our older daughter, Emily Ann, is married and lives not far from us. We see her and her husband, Larry, often.

My husband and daughters were the only people who

knew what I was doing and I want to thank them all for not asking too many questions and my husband especially for buying me a big Polish-English dictionary. (When I started to work on the translation I used a little pocket edition.) It helped me enormously.

I also want to tell you that my home is no longer El Salvador. A few months after our wedding in December of 1952 we moved to the United States. During the early years we lived in New Haven, Connecticut; Burlington, New Jersey; the Eastern shore of Virginia; Baltimore, Maryland; and for a few weeks in San Francisco, California, and New York City. We also lived on the island of Terceira in the Azores. I was happy in every place we lived—whether in a one-room apartment or an eight-room house. My dream of living in this beautiful land—the United States of America—was and is a reality.